Tantric
SUPER SEX

DUNCAN BAIRD PUBLISHERS

LONDON

Tantric

INTENSIFY YOUR LOVE LIFE WEEK BY WEEK

SUPER SEX

NICOLE BAILEY

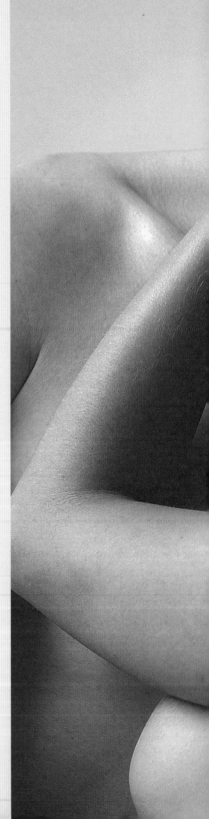

Tantric SUPER SEX
NICOLE BAILEY

Distributed in the USA and Canada by
Sterling Publishing Co., Inc.
387 Park Avenue South
New York, NY 10016-8810

First published in the UK and USA in 2010 by
Duncan Baird Publishers Ltd
Sixth Floor, Castle House, 75—76 Wells Street
London W1T 3QH

Managing Editors: Grace Cheetham and Deirdre Headon
Editor: Dawn Bates
Managing Designer: Manisha Patel
Commissioned Photography: John Davis

ISBN: 978-1-84483-904-9

10 9 8 7 6 5 4 3 2 1

Typeset in Conduit ITC
Color reproduction by Scanhouse, Malaysia
Printed in Hong Kong by Imago

For information about custom editions, special sales, premium and corporate purchases,
please contact Sterling Special Sales Department at 800-805-5489 or
specialsales@sterlingpub.com

PUBLISHER'S NOTE:
The Publisher, the author and the photographer cannot accept any responsibility for any
injuries or damages incurred as a result of following the advice in this book, or of using any
of the techniques described or mentioned herein. If you suffer from any health problems or
special conditions, it is recommended that you consult your doctor before following any
practice suggested in this book. Some of the advice in this book involves the use of massage
oil. However, do not use massage oil if you are using a condom—the oil damages latex.

contents

introduction   8

1 SENSUAL SURRENDER   10–43   **2** CONNECTING IN LOVE   44–79

the tantric way: a taste of tantra

tender embrace

position of kali

merging position

tantric technique: watching your breath

the tantric way: the chakras

love's union

the tripod

shiva on top

tantric technique: chakra breathing

pressed position

eroticizer

the tantric way: erotic sanctuary

encircling embrace

feminine essence

the tantric way: arousing sight & touch

tantric touch: fingertip touch

reclining bond

the tantric way: arousing sound, smell & taste

tantric technique: pelvic rocking

spooning embrace

the junction

close union

elephant position

the tantric way: honouring the body

fitting of the sock

sitting straddle

supported union

shakti on top

tantric technique: love muscles

sacred seat

tantric touch: three-handed massage

piercing position

raised position

open yoni

ocean of pleasure

tantric technique: heart orgasm

compact embrace

hungry tiger

3 OPENING TO ECSTASY   80–115

tantric technique: **breath of fire**
tantric technique: **kundalini shaking**
upright dog
cross-legged
ascending position
tantric touch: **yoni caress**
tantric touch: **lingam caress**
crouching dog
the pathway
lotus flower
tantric technique: **shiva dance**
tantric technique: **shakti dance**
ankle clasp
monkey embrace
tantric touch: **the sacred spot**
tantric touch: **the goddess spot**
glorious goddess
thigh grip
sitting embrace
crouching shakti
tantric technique: **female ejaculation**
standing dog
bow & arrow

4 ULTIMATE UNION   116–149

tantric technique: **soul gazing**
tantric touch: **blindfold massage**
belly dance
sitting squat
tantric touch: **the yoni kiss**
tantric touch: **the lingam kiss**
rising serpent
dog posture
yab yum
tantric technique: **circular breathing**
quiet position
lotus position
scissors
tantric technique: **the erotic servant**
star position
standing bond
tantric technique: **oil play**
mounted yantra
the clasp

further reading   150
index   150

introduction

Tantra may be thousands of years old, but its teachings still bring incredible meaning and joy to couples today. Applying Tantra to your sex life can have amazing benefits. Your connection to your lover can blossom and deepen. Sex can become ecstatic and joyful. You can become more at home in your body, and more aware of the gorgeous subtleties of sex.

There are lots of Tantric techniques and practices, but, often, Tantric sex is simply about the intentions and focus you take to bed with you. For example: your intention to lovingly honour your partner or your focus on the delicious sensations in your body as you become aroused.

WHAT IS TANTRA?

Tantra's origins are shrouded in myth, which contributes to its exotic, sexy reputation. The consensus is that it began as a spiritual path in India. The first Tantric scriptures, dated from around the 8th century, are thought to be a series of books written in the form of a conversation between the Hindu god Shiva and his female consort Shakti. A driving force behind Tantra was (and is) that enlightenment could be achieved through the sexual and spiritual union of Shiva (the masculine) and Shakti (the feminine).

DISCOVERING TANTRIC SUPER SEX

Tantric Super Sex will give you an exciting taste of Tantra. It's full of the kind of exercises that you might be taught in a Tantric workshop, but it's also packed with your favourite sex positions. With each of the 52 positions – one for each week – you'll find Tantric-inspired suggestions that will take sex to a new level. You and your lover will feel more deeply connected and more able to surrender to each other during sex.

In Chapter 1, Sensual Surrender, you'll find out about basic Tantric principles, including the chakras. You'll learn how to pull sexual energy up through your

body and how to bond with your lover through sex and massage. In chapter 2, Connecting in Love, you'll go a little deeper with techniques such as the sexy three-handed massage (see pages 68–71) and the heart orgasm (see pages 76–7), plus a range of erotic sex positions. Chapter 3, Opening to Ecstasy, invites you to lose any inhibitions and experience each other fully through intimate massage, lovemaking and dancing. Chapter 4, Ultimate Union, introduces Tantric practices such as soul gazing (see pages 118–19) and circular breathing (see pages 132–5). You'll also discover how to bring a deep Tantric experience to some of the most exciting sex positions.

To begin your Tantric journey, work through the techniques at your own pace. Don't be in a rush to achieve results . And, importantly, make a commitment to Tantric sex with your lover. Devote whole evenings to the blissful process of exploring, honouring and loving each other.

Tantric terms

CHAKRA – an energy centre in the body.

KALI – the Hindu goddess of destruction or transformation; a central figure inmany forms of Tantra.

KUNDALINI – coiled energy that lies at the base of the spine.

LINGAM – the penis. Lingam can be translated as "wand of light".

SHIVA – often used instead of the word "man" in Tantra. In Tantric mythology, Shiva is the male god who shares a divine sexual union with the goddess Shakti.

SHAKTI – often used instead of the word "woman" in Tantra. In Tantric mythology, the goddess Shakti shares a divine sexual union with the god Shiva.

YONI – the female genitals. Yoni can be translated as "sacred place" or "cave of wonder".

SENSUAL SURRENDER

chapter **1**

the tantric way
a taste of tantra

So what makes Tantric sex different from regular sex? Well, it all starts with your attitude to lovemaking. Rather than being orgasm-driven, Tantra encourages you to be meditative, aware and loving.

ENJOY SENSATIONAL SEX

Tantra teaches you to open up and to be conscious of the delicious range of physical feelings during sex. This means not just dominant sensations, such as the penis plunging into the vagina, but subtle ones too, such as the warmth of each other's skin; the pressure of her breasts; the caress of his breath. It encourages a slow and sensual approach to sex, where there's no rush to get anywhere or achieve anything. You simply surrender to the here and now and enjoy every moment of your lovemaking.

When you've honed your awareness of physical sensations, the benefits can be profound. You become more and more appreciative of small and subtle touches. Whereas once you may have needed lots of hard and fast genital friction to feel sexually excited, now a brush of your lover's lips or fingertips can make you tremble with pleasure. And something as simple as the tip of a feather brushed along your body can take you to a realm of bliss. The pleasure you once got only from your genitals can now be experienced over your entire body.

To increase your sensual awareness during lovemaking, try the exercises to "awaken the senses" on pages 38–9 and 46–7.

LOVE YOUR BODY

In Tantra you can leave behind stereotypes of physical attractiveness. The body is not only seen as divine, it's revered as a vehicle that can transport you to a higher consciousness. Although your body needs to be healthy, it doesn't have to be young, thin or beautiful. This makes it easier for

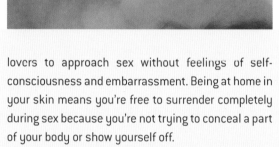

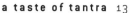

lovers to approach sex without feelings of self-consciousness and embarrassment. Being at home in your skin means you're free to surrender completely during sex because you're not trying to conceal a part of your body or show yourself off.

Through practising Tantra, you can gain a sense of pride in your body that has nothing to do with conventional standards of physical beauty. It's a great way to build your self-esteem and finally to stop wishing for a body that's better than the one you've got. This is particularly true for women, who often take the brunt of society's pressure to conform to physical stereotypes. As soon as you feel at home in your body, you'll start to sit, stand and move more confidently – and naturally exude sexiness. This reaps its own rewards: the more sexiness you put out, the more attracted people will be to you, and the more fantastic you'll feel. Try the "Body Tour" exercise on pages 55–6 to help you fall in love with your body.

savour the moment

Picture yourself drinking two glasses of fine wine. You pick up the first glass and inhale its bouquet with your eyes shut. In no rush, you put the glass to your lips and take a single sip. You hold the wine in your mouth letting the complexity of the flavours permeate your palate until you're overwhelmed by their intensity.

To drink the second glass of wine, you raise the glass to your lips and gulp the wine down, tasting it only fleetingly as it passes over your tongue.

The difference between the act of drinking the first glass of wine and the second gives you a sense of what you're aiming for in Tantra – one act is aware, present and conscious and the other isn't. The practice of Tantra helps you to operate with awareness not just during sex, but in the rest of your life, too.

"When you focus exclusively on what's happening to your body during sex, the results can be amazing. Your mind, body and spirit are as one."

STOP TRYING, START ENJOYING

Conventional sex can involve a lot of trying: trying to get aroused, trying to stay aroused, trying to reach orgasm, trying to delay orgasm, trying to give your lover an orgasm, not to mention trying to look good while all this is happening.

By contrast, Tantric sex is about letting go of sexual goals. You don't have to have a rock-hard erection that never wanes, you don't have to strive to keep your arousal at a peak and you don't have to reach orgasm every time you have sex.

Being goal-orientated means that you're never present in the moment. Instead of enjoying the journey, you're busy thinking about which route you're taking or how fast or slowly you're travelling and, as a result, missing so much pleasure.

But when you focus exclusively on what's happening to your body during sex, the results can be amazing. Your mind, body and spirit are as one, and sexual energy can flow freely through you. Instead of feeling localized sensations in your genitals, pleasure ripples through your whole body.

HONOURING RITUAL

Rituals are an important part of Tantric practice. They deepen and formalize experiences, which helps to elevate sex from the everyday to the sacred. Rituals connect you to your lover and bring a sense of specialness or spirituality to whatever you are doing. One time-honoured Tantric ritual involves preparing your room for lovemaking so that it becomes a peaceful and meditative sanctuary (see pages 34–5). Another ritual involves bowing to your partner before a Tantric sex session (see opposite). Although rituals can feel strange, funny, inappropriate or over-serious at first, it's worth getting over these feelings to discover the sense of deep connection they can bring to you and your partner.

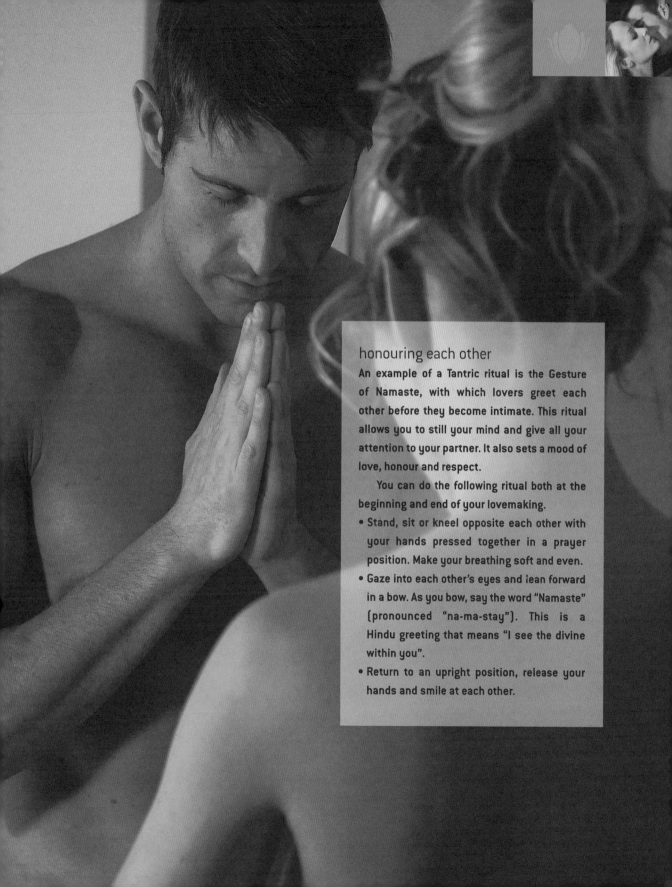

honouring each other

An example of a Tantric ritual is the Gesture of Namaste, with which lovers greet each other before they become intimate. This ritual allows you to still your mind and give all your attention to your partner. It also sets a mood of love, honour and respect.

You can do the following ritual both at the beginning and end of your lovemaking.

- Stand, sit or kneel opposite each other with your hands pressed together in a prayer position. Make your breathing soft and even.
- Gaze into each other's eyes and lean forward in a bow. As you bow, say the word "Namaste" (pronounced "na-ma-stay"). This is a Hindu greeting that means "I see the divine within you".
- Return to an upright position, release your hands and smile at each other.

tender embrace

This is an excellent position to begin your Tantric practice – after you have honoured each other with the Gesture of Namaste (see page 15), she lies back and parts her thighs, while he slides on top and gently enters her. Because you are face-to-face, you can savour the melting tenderness of being so close and intimate.

On a practical level this position is good for what ancient erotic texts describe as "high congress", which means the combination of a large penis and a small vagina. However, even if he's not well endowed and she's not compact, this position still rates high on stimulation and intensity, both physical and emotional.

Because her vagina is contracted in this position, it's a good idea for him to enter slowly so he doesn't hurt her. As well as ensuring her comfort, this is also a great way to draw out the blissful erotic tension of penetration. She, meanwhile, can concentrate on relaxing and opening up to him by breathing deeply into her genitals and letting all tension melt away from her love muscles (see page 62–5). Stay in this position for as long as you want to, but aim for at least 15–20 minutes so that you have time to tune in and open up to each other.

breath shadowing

As well as having the potential to control his arousal and prolong sex, breath shadowing is a good way of staying present during sex.

WOMEN: Try shadowing your lover's breath in this highly erotic position. Immediately after penetration, stay still, observe his breath and match your breath to his in speed, rhythm and depth. Once he starts to move in and out of you, carefully observe what happens to his breathing and breathe in the same way. His breaths will get progressively faster, and more ragged and shallow, as his excitement mounts. When you feel he's reaching a peak of excitement, stop copying his breathing and take slower, deeper breaths. See if you can lead him back down from the peak of arousal by slowing his breath down along with yours.

If your thoughts start wandering, return to breath shadowing. With practice, you'll find that breath shadowing becomes intuitive and that you'll breathe in unison.

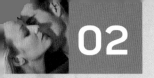

position of kali

This is named after the Indian goddess Kali. Imagine her riding on Lord Shiva with passionate, fiery energy, and you'll understand the appeal of this position.

WOMEN: Take this opportunity to unleash all your feminine power. Sit astride him and move in whatever way you wish – slide, wiggle, grind, bump, undulate or gyrate with wild abandon. If you feel self-conscious, close your eyes and allow yourself to lose control. Try to stop thinking about how you look, and whether you appear sexy or attractive. Be vocal – express yourself with deep moans or ecstatic shouts and cries.

MEN: Lie back and immerse yourself in the sights, sounds and sensations of your lover on top of you. Moan along with her.

03

merging position

In Tantric sex, the aim is to surrender completely to each other and immerse yourself in the sensations of skin on skin and breath on breath as you make love. In this position, you are intimately entwined and can enjoy a profound sense of connection.

She encloses him as deeply as possible – drawing him in, not just with her arms and legs but with her yoni (see page 9), too. Once you've got into a smooth rhythm of movement, synchronize your breathing with that of your lover (see page 17). Imagine that you're merging into a single being so that your entire awareness consists of the in- and out-flow of breath.

Take your time – there's no rush to reach orgasm. Focus instead on what's happening in the present moment – enjoy every blissful sensation of breath and movement, and the close intimacy of your naked bodies pressing against one another.

tantric technique
watching your breath

Being at one with your own body is an important part of Tantric sex and can be achieved by learning to listen to your breath. Sitting still and observing the flow of air into and out of your body can have a surprisingly profound effect.

The following breath awareness exercise not only makes you more peaceful and relaxed, it brings you home to your body. Your mind becomes still and quiet, instead of being preoccupied by thoughts such as: What time is it? What should I be doing? Literally, the only thing you need to think about is the ebb and flow of your breath. With practice, you'll discover that you don't even have to think about this. You can exist calmly and simply as a breathing body and, in this state of peaceful awareness, enjoy a blissful sexual connection with your lover.

You may struggle to maintain your focus at first, but persevere and be patient. Make a commitment to do the exercise for 10 minutes.

BREATH AWARENESS

step 1 Sit, naked, opposite your lover. Close your eyes and take as long as you need to centre yourself. Now, with your eyes open or closed, observe your next breath. Describe it to yourself. For example, is it small and tentative or fast and urgent?

step 2 Slowly deepen your breath so you pull it down deeply into the core of your body. Keep your thoughts on your breath. If your mind strays, gently bring it back – even if you have to do this every other second, persevere until you are focused on your breathing.

step 3 Make each breath deeper, fuller and more satisfying. Note any sensations in your body – such as how your belly feels as it rises and falls. Imagine the air caressing your insides.

step 4 After 10 minutes, return to breathing normally. Come "out" of your body and back into your mind and thoughts – notice the difference between the two states.

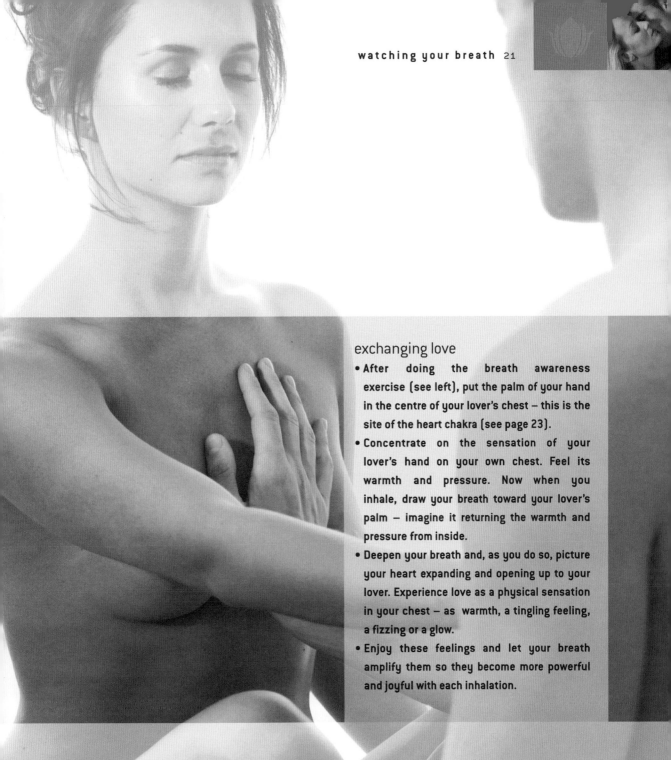

exchanging love

- After doing the breath awareness exercise (see left), put the palm of your hand in the centre of your lover's chest – this is the site of the heart chakra (see page 23).
- Concentrate on the sensation of your lover's hand on your own chest. Feel its warmth and pressure. Now when you inhale, draw your breath toward your lover's palm – imagine it returning the warmth and pressure from inside.
- Deepen your breath and, as you do so, picture your heart expanding and opening up to your lover. Experience love as a physical sensation in your chest – as warmth, a tingling feeling, a fizzing or a glow.
- Enjoy these feelings and let your breath amplify them so they become more powerful and joyful with each inhalation.

the tantric way
the chakras

As you practise Tantric sex, you'll become increasingly aware of how energy feels as it moves around your body. In particular, you may become conscious of sensations in specific places along the central core of your body. These are your chakras — centres of energy that are associated with different parts of the body, mind and spirit, and different states of being.

There are seven chakras, each of which has its own colour (see opposite) and associated benefit (see right) when energy is able to flow freely through it. All seven chakras are aligned along a vertical channel called the *sushumna*.

One of the aims of practising Tantra is to experience a state of divine oneness by raising energy from your root chakra at the bottom of the *sushumna* to the crown chakra at the top. Many of the exercises in this book require a basic knowledge of your chakras and where they're positioned along the centre of your body.

OPENING YOUR CHAKRAS

Unlock your energy to:

Gain pleasure from a strong and healthy sex drive when you unleash the sexual energy through the root chakra.

Find it easy to bond with your lover and experience joyful sexual union when energy flows freely through the sacral chakra.

Discover a strong sense of your personal power and be in charge of your emotions through your solar plexus chakra.

Feel open-hearted love and compassion through the heart chakra.

Express yourself openly when energy flows through your throat chakra.

Experience a state of peaceful mindfulness and enhanced intuition through the third eye chakra.

Enjoy a sense of oneness, merging and union when energy flows freely through the crown chakra.

the chakra map

- **The crown chakra** is at the top of your head. Linked with oneness, its colour is white.
- **The third eye chakra** lies between your eyes. Linked with peace of mind and intuition, its colour is violet.
- **The throat chakra** is in your throat. Associated with openness, its colour is blue.
- **The heart chakra** is in the centre of your chest halfway between your nipples. Linked with love and compassion, its colour is green.
- **The solar plexus chakra** is in your navel area. Linked with personal power, its colour is yellow.
- **The sacral chakra** is between your navel and genitals. Associated with attraction and sexual pleasure, its colour is orange.
- **The root chakra** is located between your anus and genitals on your perineum. Linked with sex and survival, its colour is red.

love's union

Bind yourselves closely together in this loving embrace. As you hug each other she can twine her thighs around the backs of his legs to make him feel enticingly held.

There's a tight connection between your chests, which helps you to meditate on the connection between your heart chakras (see right). You both feel so locked together, it becomes hard to sense where your physical boundaries lie.

This position is also known as Morning and Evening Prayer – it's a good way of enjoying peak connection with each other when you wake up in the morning or go to sleep at night. Because you're in a state that's halfway between sleep and waking, you're relaxed and pliable, and your mind isn't fully switched on. This makes it easier than usual to surrender yourself to sensuality. Stay in this position for as long as you want to, but try for at least 15–20 minutes so that you have time to tune in and open up to each other.

MEN: Move just enough to maintain your erection, but not so much that you ejaculate.

WOMEN: Slowly relax into this position. Close your eyes and enjoy the intimate sensation of his body on top of yours.

heart chakra meditation

As you lie together in the Love's Union position, concentrate on the feeling of your chests pressed against each other. Focus on the warmth and pressure of chest on chest, plus any subtle sensations such as his chest hair on her breasts.

Breathe in through your root chakra (see pages 28–31) and draw your breath up to the centre of your chest. Bring the sexual energy from your genitals along with it. Feel your chest opening and expanding with the breath. Breathe out through your root chakra and let go of any feelings of anger, resentment or sadness as you exhale.

Gradually synchronize your breathing so that you're both breathing into your heart chakras (see page 23). Imagine this area of your body opening up to your lover and allow a sense of softness and vulnerability to envelop you. If you like, you can focus your mind by saying the word "love" silently in your mind as you inhale.

the tripod

To give him a complete "chakra experience", try the Tripod. She starts by kneeling at his feet and taking his lingam (see page 9) into her mouth while massaging his perineum – the site of his root chakra (see page 23). He closes his eyes and concentrates on the build up of tingling sexual energy in this spot. Then, when she's ready, she moves slowly up his body kissing his belly and chest as she goes.

MEN: Imagine she's drawing sexual sensations up through your body in a line.

WOMEN: Once you've worked your way up his body, share a deep, intoxicating, mouth-to-mouth kiss with him before twining your leg around his and guiding him into you.

Depending on how close in height you are, she may need to stay still so that he doesn't slip out. If so, enjoy the intense feeling of static union – flex your love muscles (see pages 62–5) against each other.

shiva on top

Tantric techniques can breathe new life into the missionary position and make it magical again. When you're in position, concentrate on the glorious sensuality of skin on skin.

As he moves, picture the tight fit between your genitals, the alignment of your hearts, and the way your lips melt together. As well as the potential to gaze into each other's eyes and kiss in this position, you can experience an even greater sense of connection and oneness by making a seal between your lips and breathing each other's breath.

MEN: Take charge – give yourself up to sensations of strong and fiery dominance. Slide in and out of your lover so that she can feel the full length of your shaft caressing her.

WOMEN: Let your body open up to his like a flower – feel yourself letting go and completely surrendering beneath him.

tantric technique
chakra breathing

If you've practised the exercise on page 20, you'll be used to the delicious sensations of breath caressing your insides. The following exercise, which involves breathing into your chakras, feels even more sensual.

In Tantra, and other Eastern traditions, the chakras are wheels of energy that run along the midline of the body from the perineum to the crown of the head. To do this breathing exercise, you'll need an idea of where the chakras are located – look at the "map" on page 23.

DRAWING UP EROTIC ENERGY

step 1 Retreat to your erotic sanctuary with your lover. Once there, kiss, cuddle and stroke as if you're going to have sex, but instead of going all the way, ask your lover to lie down on their back and close their eyes (you can swap roles in the next session). Now use your hand to caress their genitals. Ask them to focus on the feelings of arousal building up there.

step 2 When your lover is fully turned on, press your fingers against their perineum (the area of the root chakra). They should now completely surrender to you and follow your every word. Read out the following to them: *"Breathe in and imagine you're pulling air into your body through your root chakra – exactly where my fingers are. As you breathe out, imagine the air flowing back out through this spot. Each time you inhale air through your root chakra, imagine sexual energy getting stronger and more arousing. Feel it as warmth that's getting hotter. Picture it as a red colour that's expanding and getting more intense."*

step 3 After your lover has inhaled and exhaled through the root chakra for a minute or so, move your hand in a gentle caressing movement up to their belly. Let your palm rest softly below their navel (the site of the sacral chakra). Read these instructions to them: *"Imagine a hollow tube that runs in a straight line from your root chakra to the crown of your*

head. Imagine you can pull all the tantalizing sexual feelings in your genitals up along this tube. Breathe in through your root chakra and let the sexual energy rise up through the tube to the spot where my hand is resting. Let the air flow back down through the root chakra as you breathe out. As the sexual energy rises from your genitals to your belly, picture it changing from red to orange."

PRACTISING THE TECHNIQUE

If this is the first time you've tried chakra breathing, stop at the level of the sacral chakra and keep practising what you've learned so far. Get comfortable with the idea of building up sexual feelings in your genitals and then raising them into your belly. Practise breathing in and out through your root chakra. The practices may feel strange at first and you may not feel anything, but, with practice, you will develop chakra awareness.

tips for beginners

- As your lover reads aloud the instructions, use your imagination to the full. Imagine that it's really possible to breathe in air through your root chakra. Keep your eyes closed and pour all of your attention into the sensitive spot on your perineum where your lover's fingers are touching you.

- Stay focused on the pleasure you get from chakra breathing – the aim is to expand sexual sensation so that you experience bliss throughout your whole body rather than just in your genitals.

- Trust that sensual feelings will build over time. Don't expect to feel explosive orgasms that rock your entire body – look for small, subtle feelings, such as warmth, or trickling, melting or tingling sensations. Then work on amplifying them with your breath.

When you're both learning this technique, as your lover breathes in and out, move your hand up and down their body in time with the breath. So, on each inhalation, move your hand from the root chakra up to a higher chakra and then down again. This gives your lover a tangible path to follow with their mind. When you've got to the point where raising sexual energy feels not only natural but also pleasurable and tingly, you and your lover can carry on to the next stage.

MOVING HIGHER

step 1 Repeat all the steps you've learned previously, then, after a minute or so of breathing into the sacral chakra, move your hand in a sweeping caress to the bottom of your lover's ribcage. Read aloud these instructions: *"Keep breathing in and out through your root chakra but now raise the energy as high as my hand. Imagine your breath as sexual energy that eroticizes more and more of your body as it rises.*

Feel your belly and solar plexus tingling and pulsating with sexual feelings. When your energy is level with my hand, imagine it as a yellow colour that gets stronger and more vivid with each breath."

step 2 Next, sweep your hand up to your lover's heart chakra in the middle of their chest. Continue to read aloud to your lover, as follows: *"Breathe in through your root chakra and feel the energy coming all the way up to my hand. Feel your chest opening and expanding. Feel a lovely tingling sensation where my hand is. Picture a green colour that spreads and gets stronger each time you breathe in."*

step 3 Now glide your hand up to your lover's throat and rest it there, but don't apply any pressure. Now read the following to them: *"Bring your breath as high as my hand and then let the breath flow back out through your root chakra. Feel the tingling sexual energy rise along your inner tube. Imagine it turning blue as it reaches my hand."*

"Each time you inhale air through your root chakra, imagine sexual energy getting stronger and more arousing. Feel it as warmth that's getting hotter."

step 4 Place your index and middle fingers softly between your lover's eyes – the site of their third eye chakra. Say the following: *"Breathe in all the way to my fingers. Let the breath rise smoothly all the way up from your root chakra. Bring the energy to my fingers and imagine it turning violet."*

step 5 Finally, rest your palm on the crown of your lover's head. Say: *"Breathe in through your root chakra. Pick up the sexual sensations and inhale them all the way to my hand. Let your body pulsate with bliss. Let warmth and pleasure ripple through you. Bathe in white light."*

BASKING IN PLEASURE

Lie naked together after chakra breathing. Bask in the sensations you've generated and don't rush to get up. You can swap roles so that you both have a turn at chakra breathing, or move seamlessly into making love.

pressed position

Enjoy deep, satisfying, sensual penetration in this Tantric position — also known as Totally Auspicious in the Chandamaharosana Tantra (a 9th-century Tantric scripture). She gives herself up to him and feels full from the depth of his thrusting. He feels tightly enclosed. She plants her feet on his chest as he enters her in a kneeling position.

Although he's in a dominant position, he can show his love and devotion by clasping her ankles, raising them to face level and gently kissing her soles. Licking and sucking her toes can be the finishing touch to this act of foot worship. The feeling of his penis in her vagina and her toe in his mouth, plus the exchange of some smouldering eye contact, can take you to orgasmic levels of bliss.

eroticizer

For a real spark of erotic energy, try this sensual woman-on-top position. He lies down and she climbs on top, with her legs over his shoulders, and then moves back and forth on his penis.

She can start with slow, sensual movements and then build up speed until she gets into a more rhythmic motion. He can help by moving her body with his hands. You'll get a smoother motion if you coat yourselves with massage oil beforehand.

Both imagine that the back and forth movements are generating a spark or a charge in your genitals. Then, when she stops moving, both of you can quickly contract your love muscles (see pages 62–5) and imagine the spark being propelled up through the centre of your bodies.

Take your time with this technique – try to make your muscular contractions strong and hold them for as long as possible.

the tantric way
erotic sanctuary

Turn your bedroom into a sanctuary – a place that puts you in the mood for sensual play the moment you enter. Rather than falling into bed for something fast and functional, in Tantric sex you're embarking on an experience that's special and mindful. Make the transformation of your bedroom part of your Tantric ritual. Once you've created your erotic sanctuary, slowly undress each other, and christen the room with your lover.

A HAVEN FOR LOVEMAKING

Start by clearing the room of clutter. Banish anything that reminds you of work or domestic life, plus any technology that makes an intrusive noise. If there's something about a room you don't like, such as an object that has unpleasant associations, remove it. The point of Tantric sex is to immerse yourself in the moment. If your environment contains things that distract, upset or annoy you, that immersion will be more difficult. Things that stimulate, entice and seduce make it easier. Close your eyes and imagine the smells, sounds, textures and objects you'd like in your ideal erotic environment. As far as you can, try to create this. Experiment with the following:

Light the room with soft, flickering candlelight or small lamps.

Dress your bed in clean sheets made from natural fabrics. Use woollen throws and blankets, and soft cushions for a warm, nurturing atmosphere. Keep a couple of gowns or sarongs near the bed.

Play sensual, sexy or meditative music. Depending on your taste, you could play instruments that produce a meditative sound (such as singing bowls or Tibetan cymbals), or you could have a music player set up.

Choose smells that seduce and entice – burn incense, or gardenia, sandalwood, jasmine or ylang ylang essential oils. Put your favourite sweet-smelling flowers in the room.

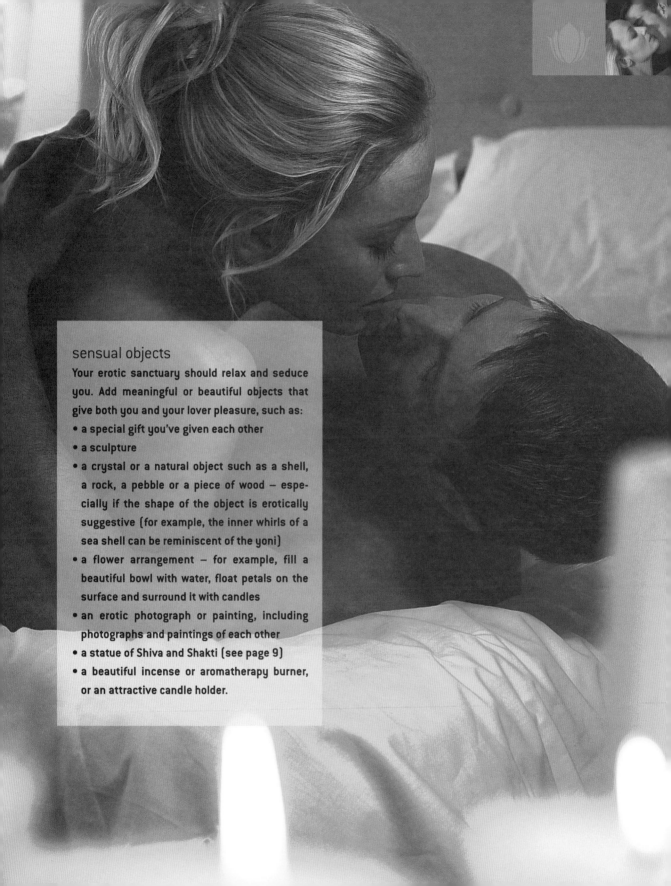

sensual objects

Your erotic sanctuary should relax and seduce you. Add meaningful or beautiful objects that give both you and your lover pleasure, such as:

- a special gift you've given each other
- a sculpture
- a crystal or a natural object such as a shell, a rock, a pebble or a piece of wood — especially if the shape of the object is erotically suggestive (for example, the inner whirls of a sea shell can be reminiscent of the yoni)
- a flower arrangement — for example, fill a beautiful bowl with water, float petals on the surface and surround it with candles
- an erotic photograph or painting, including photographs and paintings of each other
- a statue of Shiva and Shakti (see page 9)
- a beautiful incense or aromatherapy burner, or an attractive candle holder.

encircling embrace

This is perfect for practising the Tantric art of letting arousal come and go. Try to alternate periods of sexy movements with quieter, more sensual periods of kissing and cuddling. To get into position she simply wraps her legs around his body in a loose circle and presses her feet together behind his thighs.
WOMEN: During the quieter phases of sex, pull your lover's face towards yours for a passionate kiss – probe his mouth deeply with your tongue.

MEN: Instead of the thrusting or pumping movements of typical man-on-top sex, slow things down. Move smoothly inside your lover but with no intention of ejaculating. Experiment with lying completely still inside her. Use these quiet times to get in tune with your lover – watch her face, listen to her sounds and feel the small, subtle movements of her body beneath yours. If your erection disappears, don't worry – trust that it will come back again.

feminine essence

He fully surrenders to her and she explores her complete capacity for pleasure in this powerful woman-on-top position. As she flicks and undulates her hips, her vagina gets stimulated by his penis and her clitoris is massaged by his whole pubic area and the base of his shaft. She can hone her sensitivity by switching her awareness back and forth between her clitoris and her vagina.

WOMEN: Take time to focus on the different sensations that are coming from your clitoris and vagina. Feel them building up gradually – don't try to force

anything – just relax and let it happen. One of the many joys of Tantric sex is that you're under no pressure to come quickly, or at all, so just witness and savour every sensation.

MEN: Because your lover is making all the moves in this position, there's nothing to do but lie back. Watch what happens to your body as you relax into sex – you may feel intensely eroticized or you may feel you're losing arousal. Your body may jerk, tremble or convulse with pleasure or it may be still and relaxed. Observe and enjoy all your responses.

the tantric way
arousing sight & touch

Awakening the senses is a key part of Tantra – if your senses are awake, sex becomes a rich voyage of discovery in which you lovingly experience the sights, smells, sounds, touch and tastes of each other.

Spend an evening titillating your lover's sense of sight and touch. Start by laying your lover down, naked, in a warm room – either on the bed or on the floor. Ask them to give themselves up to the sensual experiences you're about to provide. To arouse their other senses, see pages 46–7.

AWAKENING SIGHT

Sex has the potential to be a visual feast – picture her nipples hardening, his penis swelling and length-ening, or the ecstatic expression on your lover's face at climax. Familiarity all too often stops us from fully seeing our lover, and when we have sex there's no longer a sense of wonder and reverence. Wake up your lover's sense of sight by undressing for them – not in a casual let's-get-down-to-business way, but with slow and deliberate erotic intent.

- Wear sensual or sexy fabrics – silk, satin or leather – that float, roll or peel away from the skin.
- Undress in a way that shows how much you adore your body. Reveal each bit of yourself as though it's a titillating treasure that your lover is privileged to see. Play music and dance if you feel like it.
- Stroke your fingers over your skin, pausing to pleasure erogenous zones and give yourself goose-bumps. Make eye contact – check that your lover is focused entirely on you.
- Once you've removed an item of clothing, let it slip onto the floor. Don't hang things up!

WAKING UP TOUCH

Kneel at your lover's head and cover their eyes with a blindfold to heighten their sensitivity to touch. Now give them an array of sensual and surprising tactile treats from the list below. But wait for a whole minute before you touch your lover and don't say anything – making them wait will cause their skin to bristle with anticipation and make that first touch all the more sensational. Try the following:

• trail a silk scarf up and down their body
• draw swirls on their skin using a feather
• plant a row of incredibly slow, soft, featherlight kisses along the length of their arm, or up their back and on to their neck
• drizzle warm massage oil on to their back
• drip wax from a massage candle onto a hairless part of their body
• crush fruit, such as strawberries or raspberries, on the front of their body
• circle their nipples with ice cubes
• tickle their belly with your hair
• stroke or spank their buttocks (but not their spine) with the back of a hairbrush.

giving and receiving

If you're doing the giving, offer your lover the gift of your undivided attention. Pour yourself into the act of performing and touching. Make it joyful. Tell your lover that, for the duration of this sensual treat, your sole purpose is to indulge, delight and serve them. Say roughly how long your sensual treat will last – 30 minutes or an hour or more – so they know they've got time to lie back and bask.

If you're the one receiving, experience the joy of seeing your lover undress for you without judgement. When you're being touched, try to suspend all thoughts about whether sensa-tions are pleasant or unpleasant (unless something actually causes pain, in which case you should ask your partner to stop immediately). Meditate on whatever experiences your lover brings to you – immerse yourself.

tantric touch
fingertip touch

You can try this amazing Tantric massage by itself or you can make it a very sexy part of your foreplay. The barely-there sensations of your fingertips on your lover's skin will create whole-body tingles.

A fingertip massage is extremely simple – you don't need any oils or other tools. All you need is a warm erotic sanctuary (see pages 34–5) and your lover's naked body. Your aim is to connect with your lover through the lightest possible touch. Using your fingertips, you can literally tap into your lover's sexual energy with electrifying results.

STARTING THE MASSAGE

step 1 Start by lying down with your lover and cuddling them. Do the breath awareness exercise (see page 20) together. Then, gently turn them on their front and kneel behind them. Place your fingertips on the back of their neck – imagine that you're trying to touch the tiny hairs on the skin rather than the skin itself. Move your hands slowly down their neck and back, keeping the touch light. If their hairs stand on end or you can see goosebumps, you know you're doing it right. If in doubt, softly whisper: "How does that feel?"

step 2 Ask your lover to lie on their front and then trail your fingers over their buttocks and the backs of their legs, all the way down to their feet (leave out the soles if your lover is ticklish). Then, use your fingertips to make big swirls and circles all over their back, keeping your touch as light as a feather.

step 3 Complete the massage by turning your lover onto their back and stroking and swirling your fingertips on the front of their body. After a while, start to linger on your lover's genitals and nipples. Tease your lover by taking your fingers away from these hotspots and then bringing them back again. When you sense your lover is buzzing with sensation, lean forward to kiss them. Then, see what happens next.

tips for beginners

- As you move your hands over your lover's skin, imagine that the tips of your fingers are buzzing with energy — picture a tiny electrical charge, a glow or a sense of heat emanating from your fingers.

- Transmit this energy to your lover as your fingers travel across their body.

- Close your eyes and intuit the places where you lover would most like to be touched. As you touch these spots, imagine them glowing and becoming warm from the power of your touch.

- If your lover isn't feeling anything, press down with your fingertips during the first round of massage, and then make your touch progressively lighter on subsequent rounds.

- Ask your lover for feedback during and after the massage.

reclining bond

This is a great introduction to a slow, sensual style of making love. If you're more used to fast roll-around-the-floor, break-out-in-a-sweat sex, this is a novel sexual experience. Although his penis fully penetrates her vagina, the connection between you is more emotional than genital.

To get into position he sits with his legs crossed (or in the lotus position if he's supple enough) and she climbs on top and wraps her legs around his waist. Now both of you lean back and take your weight on your hands.

Reclining Bond is a variation of the classic Tantric sex position known as Yab Yum (see pages 130–31). Although it's less intimate than Yab Yum, the advantage is that you can sit opposite each other in naked appreciation.

At first you may feel understimulated in Reclining Bond. You can't move very easily and neither one of you is able to call the shots and set the pace. Yet if you relax into position and accept the lack of thrusting ability, you'll gradually discover the sheer sexiness of sitting opposite each other with your eyes open. If you're feeling self-conscious or thinking "What now?" the exercise opposite will break the ice.

letting go

Being able to truly surrender to your lover is an important part of Tantra. Use the Reclining Bond positions to let go of your inhibitions. Take advantage of the fact that you're right opposite each other and there's nowhere to hide. Without feeling shy or embarrassed, let your lover see all of your body. Enjoy your own sexiness, and take in the view of your lover's naked body with candid appreciation.

Explore each other's bodies with a childlike lack of self-consciousness. Stroke and caress each other and talk as you do so – tell each other what feels good and describe why. Let your lover's descriptions turn you on. Touch different part of each other's bodies.

Keep your eyes open throughout. If you feel like smiling, laughing or giggling, go ahead. Remind yourselves that, as long as you're both enjoying the experience, there's no right or wrong way to have sex.

CONNECTING IN LOVE

chapter **2**

the tantric way
arousing sound, smell & taste

A fantastic way to truly connect with your lover is through their senses. Below is the second part of the sensory awakening ritual (see pages 38–9). Having awakened your lover's senses of sight and touch, you're now going to stimulate their senses of sound, smell and taste with an array of sensual treats.

As you did with the touch techniques, you can heighten your lover's arousal and anticipation by blindfolding them at the start of the exercise. Make sure you carry out the whole ritual in a comfortable setting, where you won't be disturbed. Tell your lover that, for the next 30 minutes or more, all they need to do is relax and give themselves up to the sensual experiences you're about to provide.

AWAKENING SOUND

Lay your lover down, naked, in a warm room — either on the bed or on some cushions or blankets on the floor. After you've treated your lover to a massage, or some kisses and caresses, play or perform a sequence of sounds to them.

Ask your lover to relax and to let the sounds enter them. Try a range of intoxicating or resonant sounds, such as:

- a drum beat that starts slowly and softly and then gets progressively faster, louder and wilder
- a recording of waves crashing on the shore
- your own breath taken deeply into your body and released slowly and calmly
- a recording of birdsong
- your voice chanting the sacred syllable "om"
- a piece of classical, sensual, atmospheric or meditative music
- an instrument, such as a singing bowl (see page 34) or a bell, that has a lingering resonance. Play the instrument while walking around your lover so they feel enclosed in a circle of sound.

AWAKENING SMELL

After a minute has passed, ask your lover to re-tune their awareness to their sense of smell. Pass a selection of smells beneath their nostrils. Ask them to inhale each one deeply and then exhale fully. Allow 10 breaths between each smell so that each one is fully absorbed. Try any of these:

• incense, scented candles or an essential oil, for example, ylang ylang, rose or jasmine
• fresh flowers or herbs
• a home-made cake or freshly baked bread
• a freshly cut lemon
• a recently extinguished candle
• coconut oil rubbed into your lover's skin or hair
• a drop of perfume dabbed somewhere on your naked body – ask your lover to explore you to discover the exact site of the scent.

You can also ask your lover to imagine smells, for example, a fragrant pine forest, an ocean breeze, chestnuts roasting in a fire, or the scent of a flower garden after rain.

AWAKENING TASTE

Finally, you're going to indulge your lover's taste buds with tiny morsels of intensely flavoured foods. Tell your lover that their role is not to guess what the food is, but simply to experience its flavour in all its fullness and richness. As always, take your time and leave a gap between each food. Offer any of the food and drinks listed below to your lover:

• one bite of a ripe and juicy peach or mango
• your finger dipped into some liqueur and gently stroked onto your lover's tongue
• a fragment of the darkest chocolate
• a small sip from a glass of full-bodied red wine (or drizzle wine from your mouth to theirs)
• a thread of honey dripped onto your lover's outstretched tongue.

tantric technique
pelvic rocking

Try this sexy Tantric exercise with your lover – it helps you to build up erotic energy. When you're used to pelvic rocking, you can try it during sex.

ROCK TOGETHER

step 1 Kneel or stand opposite each other (if you stand, keep your knees slightly bent and your feet apart). With your spine straight and your belly relaxed, start to rock your pelvis backward and forward (but not up and down). Don't worry about synchronizing your movements with one other – just concentrate on getting the movement right at this stage. Try to isolate your pelvis so that, as you rock, the rest of your body stays still – there shouldn't be any movement in your legs, chest or shoulders.

step 2 Get into a natural and rhythmic flow of movement and when you feel ready, start to coordinate your breath with your movement: inhale as you rock your pelvis backward and exhale as you rock

forward. Again, don't worry about what your lover is doing – just allow yourself to get enjoyably lost in the rhythm of the movement.

step 3 Keep up this combination of breath and movement for several minutes. Be aware of any sensations in your perineum, genitals or pelvis – feelings of warmth, melting or tingling. Focus on these feelings, and let them become more expansive. If you like, you can now add one further action to the breath/movement rhythm: squeeze your love muscles (see pages 62–5) on each backward rock and release them on each forward rock.

step 4 When it feels right, make eye contact with your lover. As soon as they return your gaze, start to synchronize your movements so you both inhale and rock back at the same time, then both exhale and rock forward. Again, get a rhythmic flow of movement going that feels easy and natural. Let a deep, wordless connection develop between you.

rock with pleasure

Pelvic rocking helps sex to become more pleasurable and sensual in a number of ways.

- Rocking makes you more flexible in your pelvis, hips and sacrum, so you can move more freely and fluidly during sex.
- Rocking helps you let go of tension in your lower back and abdomen, making this area feel relaxed and open to sexual sensation.
- If you rock your pelvis during lovemaking (as shown here), it helps to generate and expand sexual energy throughout your body.
- Rocking brings your awareness to your perineum, genitals and pelvis, and makes you more conscious of sensation and energy in this part of your body.
- The repetitive, rhythmic movement of pelvic rocking helps you and your lover to get into a meditative state during lovemaking.

spooning embrace

You can relax and explore sexual sensation in a slow and leisurely way in the Spooning Embrace. Although it's easy for him to thrust quickly from behind, experiment with slower, gentler movements. Try staying still and flexing your love muscles against each other. Take turns to rock your pelvis back and forth. Try simultaneous slow rocking. Even if you crave hard and fast genital stimulation, stay with the gentle mood and see where it takes you. If you're feeling extremely aroused and close to orgasm, try this Tantric technique to help you last longer: pour your attention into a part of your body you wouldn't normally consider sexual, such as your belly or your throat. See if you can move the arousal from your genitals to this place. If you can, see if you can move it on further to a second destination.

the junction

This is another laidback, restful position for slow-paced lovemaking. It's easy for her to touch herself because she's got unimpeded hand-to-clitoris access and she can open her legs wide if she wants to.

WOMEN. Take the opportunity to lie back and relax into the eroticism of bespoke clitoral stimulation combined with a vaginal massage from his penis. Once you've built up a hub of sexual excitement, play around with the sensations – try tensing your vaginal muscles or letting them relax completely. Observe the effects. Try different types of breath – fast panting or slow, deep breathing. Become an expert in what ramps up or dampens down your arousal.

MEN: Let your lover explore her own sensations in this position. Enjoy watching her body as it contracts and relaxes with erotic joy.

close union

In Tantric sex you take time to experiment – the smallest change to a position can have wonderful effects. Close Union is similar to Feminine Essence (see page 37), but instead of having her legs on the outside of his, they're tucked inside.

This small difference can act as a big sensation enhancer, because it increases the pressure on her clitoris and makes him feel more tightly gripped. It can also make orgasm more likely for her – some women find it easier to come with their legs together.

WOMEN: Try shaking your pelvis in this position. Imagine that you're shaking his lingam inside you. This provides both of you with fast vibrations that feel fantastic and also frees up your pelvis and gets energy moving along your chakras (see pages 22–3). It's especially good for opening your sacral chakra. (If shaking feels good, try the exercise on pages 84–5.)
MEN: Focus on the glorious sensations rippling through your lingam. Relax completely as your lover shakes and trembles on top of you.

elephant position

This is a lovely way to have restful rear-entry sex. Whereas other rear-entry positions invite fast thrusting, Elephant Position allows you to take a slower, more connected Tantric approach. Even though you can't gaze into each other's eyes, you can immerse yourselves in sound and touch: whisper and moan softly to one another; and relish the sensation of his lingam fitting snugly in her yoni.

MEN: Explore different types of movement in this position. Try plunging deep for a couple of strokes and then bobbing in the shallow end of her yoni. Observe the effect on your arousal levels — find out what takes your lust levels higher and what keeps you on a plateau. It's useful information when you're trying to delay ejaculation.

If you like position changes during sex, Elephant lends itself to rolling over. Side-by-side sex and woman-on-top sex are just a spin away. Or try just rolling for the sake of it — enjoy the flowing movements. Treat it as adult playtime.

the tantric way
honouring the body

Tantric sex can connect you deeply with your lover, but first you both need to feel at ease with your bodies. You may feel fine jumping into bed and having sex under the sheets, or in the dark, but less happy standing naked in front of a lover. If there's any part of your body you dislike or reject – or if you hate your appearance, full stop – it's difficult to surrender unconditionally to your lover. This is where the following rituals can help: through a slow and gentle process they allow you to open up and be vulnerable.

The aim of each ritual is to let your lover know that you love and accept their body, and that you feel your body is loved and accepted, too. Although you can do each ritual by itself, it's helpful to do them as a sequence so that you're relaxed and intimate before the final genital-honouring ritual.

Take it in turns to lead each other through the sequence. When you're the one who is leading, treat it as an opportunity to meditate on your lover's body and witness any positive or negative thoughts you have about it. You may feel as though you should suppress critical or judgemental thoughts so that you don't subtly convey them to your lover. Instead, allow all thoughts to arise and disappear again. Eventually, you'll emerge into a space where you can simply be with your lover with a feeling of joy.

RITUAL 1: WATER MASSAGE
Fill the bath with hot water and add a few drops of jasmine or your favourite essential oil. Light candles and put them around the edge of the bath.

When your lover is lying in the water, ask them to close their eyes and tell them you're going to massage them with water. As they receive the massage, ask them to rotate their awareness through these four senses:

• hearing (the sound of water gently trickling and splashing)

- smell (the scent of jasmine or other essential oil)
- touch (the sensation of hot water against skin)
- sight (the flicker of candlelight beneath closed eyelids).

Dip a sponge in the bathwater, hold it a little way from your lover and gently squeeze out the water over their neck, shoulders and chest. Gently lift one foot out of the water at a time and use the sponge to drizzle water over the toes and the soles of their feet. Do the same with your lover's hands and arms, concentrating on the palms and forearms. (Don't lift their legs and their arms if you can't completely support their weight – the massage won't have the same effect if your lover has to do the work.)

Keep up the massage so there's an almost constant flow of water against the skin. Allow your lover to sink into a deep relaxation. When they're ready to come out of the bath, greet them with a towel that's big enough to enclose their whole body. Once

they're warmly wrapped up, spend some time kissing and cuddling them in the steamy bathroom. Then take your lover's hand and lead them to the bedroom for the next stage of the ritual.

RITUAL 2: BODY TOUR

Stand in front of a full-length mirror with your naked lover so that you're embracing them from behind and they can see the reflection of the front of their body. Ask your lover to tell you the story of their body by describing all its different parts. For example, "These are my breasts: they're quite small; the left one is bigger than the right one."

Ask your lover to be descriptive, but to avoid using any negative words such as "ugly" or negative phrases such as "I hate". If they find this difficult, ask them to pretend that they're they describing a figure in a painting – concentrating on details such as colour, texture, size and shape, but without

"The aim of the rituals is to let your lover know that you love and accept them, and to help your lover accept and love their own body."

evaluation. The aim is for your lover to suspend criticism and judgement and to concentrate on impartial description.

As your lover tells you the story of their body, cuddle them and listen to their descriptions. After they've "toured" the front of their body, get them to turn around and do the same thing from other angles. After this, kiss your lover's body from head to toe.

RITUAL 3: HONOURING THE GENITALS

Many people have a deep-rooted sense of shame about their genitals, yet, in Tantra the male and female genitals are revered as sacred. Although it may seem strange to simply look at your lover's genitals, it can be a liberating experience.

Ask your lover to lie back on cushions, and open their legs so that you can see the length of her vulva or his penis, scrotum and perineum. Instead of reaching out to touch, caress and stimulate, as you might usually, simply let your gaze rest on your lover's genitals. Explore and absorb your lover's genitals through your eyes, observing any thoughts that come to mind. Let whatever comes into your mind – everything from desire, curiosity and appreciation to distaste, guilt, and feelings of voyeurism and curiosity – come and go. Gaze at your lover in this way for 10–20 minutes, then lovingly embrace them.

When it's your turn to receive your lover's gaze, observe your thoughts in the same way as you did when you were the "looker". Accept any feelings you have of shame, exposure, silliness or embarrassment and wait for them to pass. Visualize your genitals as a sacred source of life.

CLOSE BONDING

When you've done the three-part ritual, lie comfortably in each other's arms. If you feel sexy, make love in a mood of total love and acceptance of each other.

fitting of the sock

He can take the time to really make love to her in this position and she can lie back and soak up all the sensual pleasure. As well as being a highly erotic sex position, you can use Fitting of the Sock for yoni massage (see pages 90–91), too.

MEN: Before you penetrate her in this position, take advantage of the fact that you can heighten arousal for both of you by massaging her with the tip of your penis. Put a dab of lube on her vaginal entrance, then hold your shaft firmly in your hand and use the glans to spread the lube over her genitals, as though you're painting her. As things get hotter, use your glans to draw circles around her clitoris getting progressively harder and faster. When you finally penetrate her, the sensation will be electrifying. Tip: if you give her a yoni massage in this position, put plenty of cushions or pillows under the small of her back so she's free to let go completely.

sitting straddle

This sitting position is perfect for building an erotic Tantric connection – it's intimate, you're facing each other and you can make sexual energy rise through your chakras by rocking against one another (see pages 48–9). You can do Sitting Straddle on a chair, a sofa or on the edge of the bed. She can adapt her leg position to whatever form of furniture you're using.

Enjoy the blissful sensations of energy expanding through your bodies as you make love in Sitting Straddle. Visualize a sun in your pelvis – as you get more and more aroused, picture the sun shining more brightly and radiating more and more heat. Imagine this heat spreading up through your body and inflaming both of you.

supported union

This is an easier version of Standing Bond (see page 144): it gives you the erotic frisson of having vertical sex but without him having to support her weight. Find the right height surface — table, kitchen counter or chest of drawers — then take up your positions.

Use this position to enjoy a blissful Tantric kiss as he moves inside her. A Tantric kiss is simply one in which you stay present with each sensation as it occurs. You can make the kiss slow and tentative, wild and greedy or soft and sensual — but whatever you do, give it your whole-hearted attention. If you find your mind wandering, bring yourself — and your lover — back by trying a new kissing technique. For example, suck the tip of your lover's tongue, nibble and suck each other's lips, flick your tongues, or simply rest your parted lips against your lover's, close your eyes and swoon.

shakti on top

The fronts of your bodies are pressed close in this intimate bond. Because you can't make big or fast movements in this position, it's ideal for Tantric meditation. Play some sensual music that you both love and then pour your awareness into the music and let it enhance the connection between the two of you. Check that your bodies are relaxed — inhale simultaneously and let your breath dissolve any areas of tension. Gradually let yourself go into a deeper relaxation, visualizing your minds and bodies becoming fluid and intertwined.

If you struggle with this meditation because you feel sexually frustrated and under-stimulated and/or you can't relax, try mixing periods of movement with periods of stillness. For example, she can sit up and move vigorously, then lie down and breath in time with him, and so on.

tantric technique
love muscles

You can truly connect with each other by working your love muscles during sex. Also known as pelvic floor or pubococcygeal muscles, these play an important role in Tantric sex – contracting and relaxing them is an ancient technique that helps you to build sexual energy in your genitals.

LOCATING YOUR LOVE MUSCLES

It's easy to locate your love muscles – they're the ones you clench when you're trying not to urinate or when you're trying to stop the flow mid-pee. Strengthening them can enhance sexual sensation: during orgasm the love muscles contract rhythmically, so the stronger the muscles, the stronger the sensations.

Exercises involving love muscle contractions have always been practised in yoga and Tantra. And they're considered just as important for men as they are for women. If you go to yoga classes, you may have been instructed to contract "mulabandha"

or your "root lock" to contain energy within your body. In Tantric sex, love muscle exercises help to power the circulation of sexual energy up through *sushumna* (the hollow tube you visualized in the chakra breathing exercise – pages 28–9). This moves eroticism beyond your genitals and throughout your body, so that whole-body orgasms become possible.

WORKING YOUR LOVE MUSCLES

step 1 To work on your love muscles, begin by lying on your back in a comfortable place. Practise the breath awareness exercise on page 20 to still your mind and bring you into your body. When you're ready, breathe in and contract your love muscles. Try to contract them in isolation – don't tense your buttock and abdominal muscles too. This gets easier the more you practise. As you exhale, release your muscles completely. Make a sound such as "aahhhhhh" if it helps you to let go.

step 2 Pause after a few contractions to note the feelings in your body. Don't worry if you don't feel much when you exercise your love muscles: if you keep practising in a spirit of curiosity and self-acceptance, you'll be able to develop the full potential of this part of your body.

step 3 (optional) Try working your love muscles in a different position to see if you get a stronger sensation. For example, try lying on your back and bending your knees with your feet on the floor, or try a deep squat with your heels on the ground and your knees apart. Or you may find sitting on a hard chair helpful.

USING YOUR LOVE MUSCLES

Try to practise love muscle contractions at least once a day for several minutes at a time. Once you've developed an awareness of your love muscles, you can use them to stimulate your partner during

total love muscle release

If you regularly work your love muscles (see left), you'll probably have trained yourself to concentrate on the upward contractions rather than the downward relaxations. However, from a Tantric point of view, releasing muscle tension is very important. With this in mind, try adding the following stage to your exercises: as you breathe out, relax your love muscles completely then bear down slightly (this time, imagine that you're trying to push urine out rather than hold it in).

By mastering total love muscle release, you can experience wonderful sensations during sex. It can lead to a feeling of truly letting go and surrendering to a lover. There's another sexy bonus to bearing down – it may help some women to ejaculate after G-spot stimulation (see pages 106–7).

sex (see below). You can also combine love muscle contractions with pelvic rocking (see page 48) and breathing to draw up sexual energy and experience sensual ripples through your whole body.

THE SECRET LANGUAGE

The "secret language" is a term coined by Tantric teachers Michaels and Johnson. It describes a Tantric style of lovemaking in which you use your love muscles to stimulate each other, but remain otherwise still. Viewed externally it looks like nothing is going on. Internally, you're busy firing each other up with hot erotic energy.

To master the secret language, work on contracting and relaxing your love muscles every day. As this gets easier, introduce more complexity — try pulsing or fluttering your love muscles, too.

When you've fine-tuned your muscle control, try having sex in which you abandon the conventional in-out movements of the penis in the vagina and stimulate each other with internal movements instead. He'll feel her muscle contractions as a squeezing pressure along the length of his shaft. She'll feel his contractions as pressure against her vaginal wall. Take turns to "speak" (treat it as a conversation between your muscles). For example: he does three fast pulses and three slow ones; then she replies with the same.

Play around with different speeds and rhythms. Treat this as a fun and playful way to tease and stimulate each other, but use it also as a meditative exercise in which you breathe in time with each other, soul gaze (see pages 118–19) and bask in external stillness and relaxation.

AROUSAL UPS AND DOWNS

If you abandon external movement during sex and rely solely on the secret language, you'll

probably notice your arousal levels going up and down. Periods of intense excitement may be followed by periods where you just feel like resting in each other's arms. In Tantric sex, this is completely normal and reflects waves of active male energy alternating with quieter, more receptive female energy. However, many men – and their lovers – tend to panic, believing that something is wrong if they lose their erection during sex. This prompts men to return to hard thrusting to get their erection back.

Although pumping, grinding and thrusting can successfully maintain your arousal levels and keep you on the road to orgasm, it can stop you experiencing the depth, and the rich, sensual union of the quieter moments. If you're making love using only the secret language, don't aim for a rock-hard penis. In fact, embrace the idea that his erection will disappear – it gives you both a fantastic chance to rest in glorious and sensual feminine energy.

"There may be periods of intense excitement, and periods where you just feel like resting in each other's arms. In Tantric sex, this is completely normal."

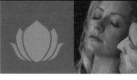

sacred seat

He sits with his legs straight out in front while she takes a seat on his lap with her back to him. Once she's kneeling astride him, she leans forwards to rest her hands on his knees. This gives him a chance for complete Tantric immersion in the visual aspects of sex – he can feast his eyes on the erotic curve of her buttocks and the way her yoni caresses his shaft as she moves on him.

Because his lingam bends away from his body in Sacred Seat, there's a tendency for him to slip out during sex. She can prevent this by keeping her movements small, staying close to him and grinding in circles rather than bobbing up and down. She can also try pelvic shaking in this position – her rapid movements will send vibrations of pleasure through the genitals for both of you and get kundalini energy rising through her body (see pages 82–5).

You can experiment with different angles in this position. The most extreme angle is him flat on his back and her leaning so far forward that her head is between his feet. Try variations to find out what feels most comfortable and pleasurable for you.

mid-sex cuddle

Take a mid-sex break during Sacred Seat so you can relax in an erotic cuddle. She sits up so her back is against his front, and then he wraps his arms round her in a close embrace.

MEN: Rest your chin on her shoulder and nuzzle her neck and ear lobe. Seduce her with the gentle touch of your breath – let it caress her ear. WOMEN: Harmonize your breath with his.

Meditate on the fact that you're so intimately joined, both externally and internally. If your thoughts wander, bring them back to the contact points between your two bodies: her thighs on his; his lingam enclosed in her yoni; his belly and chest pressing against her back; his arms around her. Picture these contact points becoming blurry so it's hard to tell where one of you ends and the other begins.

tantric touch
three-handed massage

During a conventional massage you'd probably rely on your hands alone to stroke and caress your partner's body. In this three-handed Tantric massage you have an extra tool or "hand" at your disposal: your penis or vagina. As your hands caress your lover's body, your penis or vagina penetrates or encloses them. This simple yet powerful idea was originated by Tantric massage therapist Kenneth Ray Stubbs – it's a great way to take your lover to a peak of sexual arousal and whole-body sensuality.

The following instructions are for a three-handed massage from a man to a woman. Women, turn the page ...

THREE-HANDED TOUCH FOR HER

step 1 Assuming she's on her back, kneel between her legs and smooth warm massage oil into the front of her body. Let your palms glide and slide over her belly and breasts, including her nipples. Extend your caresses to her shoulders, arms and sides, and ask her if she'd prefer your touch to be stronger or lighter.

step 2 As your lover relaxes, glide your hands over her belly and along her thighs. As your hands pass her genitals, let your fingers stray teasingly onto her pubic area and vulva. Touch her inner thighs lightly. When the time seems right, start to stroke and caress her yoni with your palms and fingertips.

step 3 Return to stroking the front of her body and let your penis nudge her genitals as you lean over her, and naturally find its way to her vaginal entrance. Slowly penetrate her – your aim is to keep her in a state of delicious sensual relaxation rather than to make her energized with hard and fast thrusting.

step 4 Move your hands and penis as though they're joined; all three "hands" should move in slow and sensual union. Your hands stroke her breasts and belly while your penis strokes her insides. Visualize sexual energy flowing out of your "hands" and into her body.

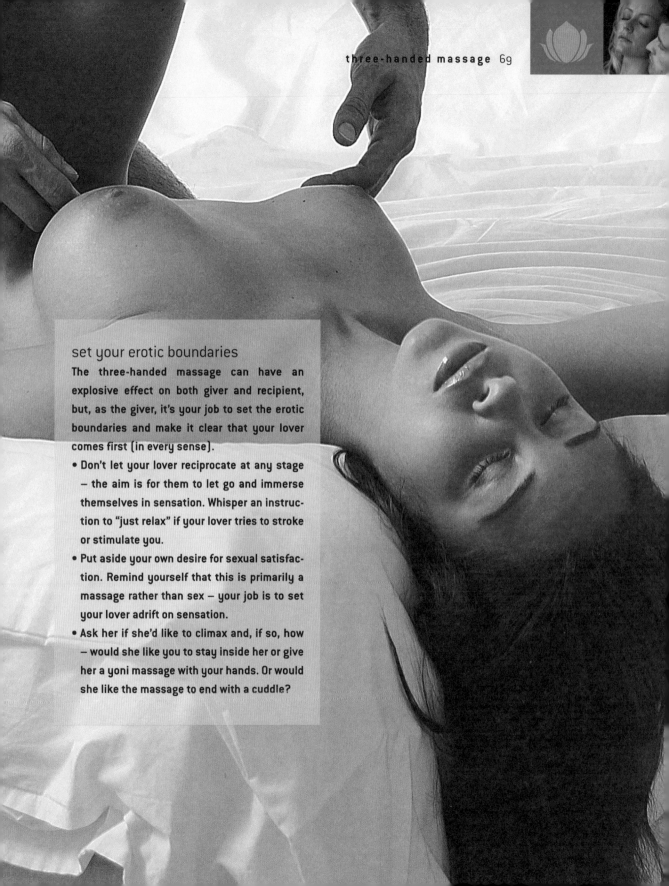

set your erotic boundaries

The three-handed massage can have an explosive effect on both giver and recipient, but, as the giver, it's your job to set the erotic boundaries and make it clear that your lover comes first (in every sense).

- Don't let your lover reciprocate at any stage – the aim is for them to let go and immerse themselves in sensation. Whisper an instruction to "just relax" if your lover tries to stroke or stimulate you.

- Put aside your own desire for sexual satisfaction. Remind yourself that this is primarily a massage rather than sex – your job is to set your lover adrift on sensation.

- Ask her if she'd like to climax and, if so, how – would she like you to stay inside her or give her a yoni massage with your hands. Or would she like the massage to end with a cuddle?

THREE-HANDED TOUCH FOR HIM

Women, now it's your turn to give him the delights of the three-handed massage.

step 1 Get him to lie down on his back and ask him to relax completely.

step 2 Straddle his waist so your genitals are close to his and put your oiled hands flat on his chest. Lean forward so some of your weight is resting on his body and then glide your hands in circles all over his chest, nipples and shoulders. Make your strokes stronger or milder depending on his feedback. Let your genitals brush his penis as you move.

step 3 As you feel him warming to your touch, shift your weight back and start to include his penis and balls in your massage. At first just brush them lightly with your fingers as your hands slide up and down. Tease him with fleeting touches and then pay more attention to his penis, taking it in your hands and stroking the shaft smoothly (see pages 92–3).

step 4 Move back up his body so you're straddling his waist, and massage his chest with your breasts. Let the tip of his penis nudge your vagina, then, when you're ready, slide onto the length of his shaft to enclose him completely. Now, massage the front of his body with your hands. Build up a flowing movement in which your hands and yoni are working in fluid harmony. As your hands glide up his body, let his lingam slip out of you slightly. On the downward movement, sink onto his shaft to enclose him completely.

Concentrate on giving him an intensely sensual experience and resist the urge to speed up your movements, or move in a way that stimulates you rather than him. If he loses his erection, don't let it deter you. Carry on with the massage using your vulva rather than your vagina as your third "hand".

step 5 Let him choose how the massage ends. Offer to bring him to orgasm through sex or manual massage or to lie blissfully entwined with him.

"Concentrate on giving
him an intensely sensual
experience and resist the
urge to speed up or move
in a way that stimulates
you rather than him."

piercing position

This position offers incredible passion and intensity. The challenge in Tantric terms is to harness your sexual energy and give each other a lingering erotic treat. Try to make the intensity smoulder and burn for as long as you can. One way to do this is to start in the missionary position and gradually go higher until her knees are by her nipples.

WOMEN: Inch your legs slowly up his body until they're hooked over his shoulders.

MEN: Don't shrink from your dominant role – enjoy it. Relish your potency and power. Express yourself vocally by moaning, growling or panting. Try to keep your buttocks relaxed as you move. It's common for men to clench their buttocks when they're on top, with the result that sexual tension and momentum builds up quickly leading to an explosive ejaculation. You can reverse this and enjoy slower and more sensual Tantric-style lovemaking by consciously relaxing.

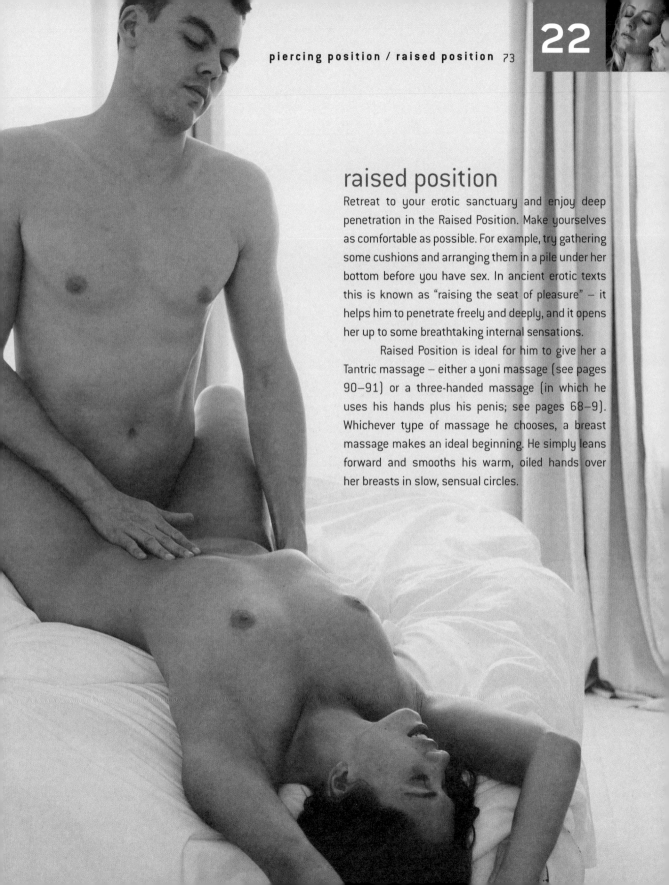

raised position

Retreat to your erotic sanctuary and enjoy deep penetration in the Raised Position. Make yourselves as comfortable as possible. For example, try gathering some cushions and arranging them in a pile under her bottom before you have sex. In ancient erotic texts this is known as "raising the seat of pleasure" – it helps him to penetrate freely and deeply, and it opens her up to some breathtaking internal sensations.

Raised Position is ideal for him to give her a Tantric massage – either a yoni massage (see pages 90–91) or a three-handed massage (in which he uses his hands plus his penis; see pages 68–9). Whichever type of massage he chooses, a breast massage makes an ideal beginning. He simply leans forward and smooths his warm, oiled hands over her breasts in slow, sensual circles.

open yoni

Her legs are wide open in erotic invitation as he climbs on top to enter her. This position can be super-arousing for both of you, especially if he gazes at her yoni before he penetrates and/or pleasures her with his tongue. As you make love concentrate on your penis and vagina respectively. After orgasm (his, hers or both) rest in each other's arms. She can wrap her legs behind his back to make him feel tightly held.

WOMEN: Imagine that you are sucking heat and eroticism from his penis. Take the sensations deeply into your vagina — let the heat inflame you and drive your passion higher.

MEN: Imagine your penis pulsating with love as you move inside her. Imagine filling her with love and energy on each thrust.

ocean of pleasure

This extremely sexy position is a Tantric treat for the eyes — you may not be able to see each other's faces but you can angle your heads to see the erotic seal between your bodies. Ocean of Pleasure is also an excellent way of giving her a three-handed back massage (see page 68). She can allow her body to relax as she leans forward and uses his legs for support. He, meanwhile can flex his penis inside her, while massaging her back.

MEN: Rub warm massage oil into the length of her back, then try a variety of hand strokes: flat hand-over-hand stroking; drawing your fingertips in a firm line on either side of her spine; clawing with your fingers; and a light barely-there touch (see page 40). Move from firm strokes to soft ones.

tantric technique
heart orgasm

Combine this wonderful Tantric breathing exercise with pleasuring yourself and you might just experience a heart orgasm. Before you try this technique, it's a good idea to practise the chakra breathing exercise (see page 28) a few times. Because you're going to be drawing up energy to your heart chakra, you need to be familiar with the practice of pulling up sexual energy along your central channel.

STEPS TO A HEART ORGASM

step 1 Lie or sit down in a comfortable position and start to stroke and caress your genitals. Go slowly and experiment with different types of touch. Let your thoughts linger on a favourite sexual fantasy. Tease yourself: move your hands away occasionally to explore other pleasure zones.

step 2 When you're feeling extremely turned on, start to stimulate your genitals in earnest, as though you're aiming to have an orgasm. Then, at the last moment – just before you come – take your hand away from your genitals and sweep your palm up the centre of your body to the centre of your chest (the site of your heart chakra – see page 23). At the same time take a fast inhalation of air (fill your lungs), hold your breath and tightly contract your love muscles (see pages 62–5). Visualize all the intense and hot sexual feelings moving up in a straight line from your genitals to your heart.

step 3 Hold your breath and the muscle contraction for as long as feels comfortable. Feel your chest expand with tingling warmth (the more you practise this technique, the stronger your heart orgasm will become). Then, exhale and relax your love muscles. At the same time, sweep your hand back down from your heart to your genitals, moving all the sexual energy back down with it. Try this exercise several times in a row before abandoning yourself to a powerful genital orgasm, if you wish to.

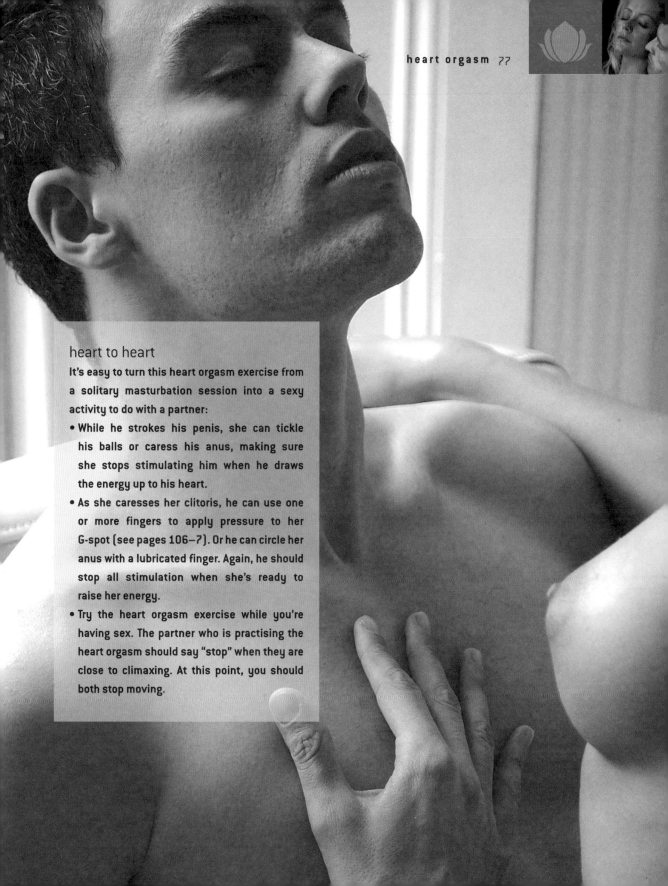

heart to heart

It's easy to turn this heart orgasm exercise from a solitary masturbation session into a sexy activity to do with a partner:

- While he strokes his penis, she can tickle his balls or caress his anus, making sure she stops stimulating him when he draws the energy up to his heart.

- As she caresses her clitoris, he can use one or more fingers to apply pressure to her G-spot (see pages 106–7). Or he can circle her anus with a lubricated finger. Again, he should stop all stimulation when she's ready to raise her energy.

- Try the heart orgasm exercise while you're having sex. The partner who is practising the heart orgasm should say "stop" when they are close to climaxing. At this point, you should both stop moving.

compact embrace

Celebrate the combination of intimacy and eroticism in this position by holding each other tenderly. Stroke each other's faces with your hands and whisper loving words softly to each other. This is a wonderful position to gaze into each other's eyes and truly connect.

She keeps her legs together in this variation of the missionary position, which means the fit between your genitals is deliciously snug. His shaft rubs her clitoris in parallel movements, which can help take her to the peak of arousal

MEN: As you're making love, try pulling out almost to the point of withdrawal on each stroke, then enter your lover again with exquisite slowness, all the time gazing into her eyes.

WOMEN: Imagine you're sucking him in and hold his gaze as he makes love to you.

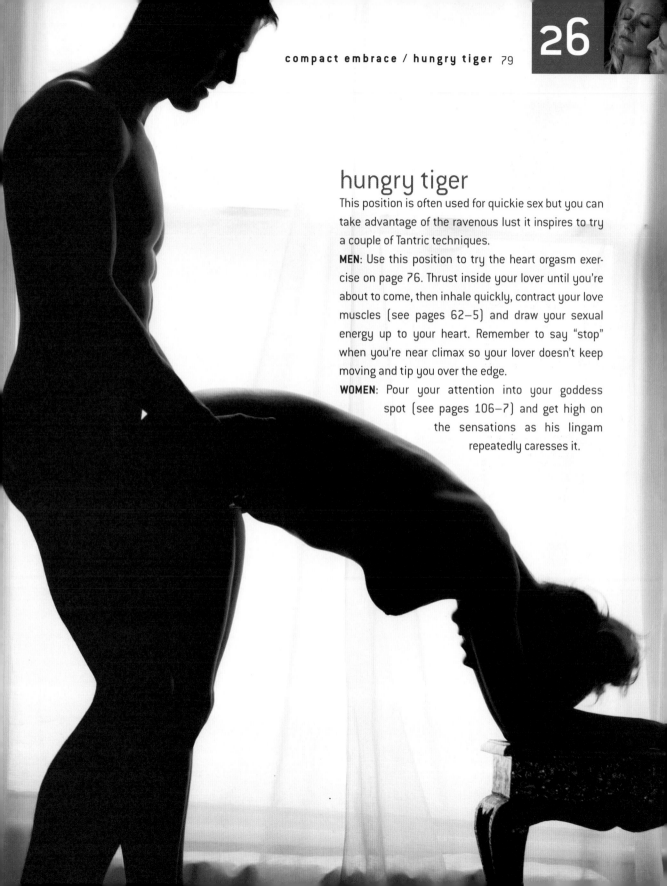

hungry tiger

This position is often used for quickie sex but you can take advantage of the ravenous lust it inspires to try a couple of Tantric techniques.

MEN: Use this position to try the heart orgasm exercise on page 76. Thrust inside your lover until you're about to come, then inhale quickly, contract your love muscles (see pages 62–5) and draw your sexual energy up to your heart. Remember to say "stop" when you're near climax so your lover doesn't keep moving and tip you over the edge.

WOMEN: Pour your attention into your goddess spot (see pages 106–7) and get high on the sensations as his lingam repeatedly caresses it.

OPENING TO ECSTASY

chapter **3**

tantric technique
breath of fire

Try this powerful kundalini yoga (see page 84) technique to open your energy channels and feel hot and tingling all over. As with Tantra, the aim of kundalini yoga is to awaken a state of deep joy by raising energy through your chakras. If you do Breath of Fire before you have sex, it will make you feel wide awake and literally "fired up". It also feels fantastic if you try this technique in the middle of lovemaking.

You can do Breath of Fire with your lover, but unlike other Tantric breathing exercises, you don't need to synchronize your breath with your lover's. Sit cross-legged on the floor with your spine straight and take a few normal breaths before you begin.

PANT ...

To practise the forceful exhalations of the Breath of Fire technique, try doing some panting breaths beforehand. Simply stick out your tongue and start panting like a dog. Pull your navel rapidly towards your spine as you exhale – you're trying to force the air out of your body as fast as you can. If you put your palm on your abdomen, you should feel your belly and diaphragm pulsating rapidly.

... AND THEN SPREAD THE FIRE

Now you've tried panting, move on to the Breath of Fire technique itself. Withdraw your tongue and close your mouth. Do the same forceful exhalations as you did before, but this time through your nose. Build up your breathing into a fast and powerful rhythm. If it helps, visualize your abdomen as a pair of bellows. Get a sense of heat emanating from your solar plexus (see page 23) and spreading through your body.

If you're doing Breath of Fire correctly, you should find you don't need to pay any attention to your inhalations – they just happen naturally. This is because, as you relax your diaphragm, the air automatically rushes back in to fill your lungs.

tips for beginners

- Make your breaths continuous. Try not to pause between exhalations and inhalations.
- Be aware that you may not feel all of the invigorating benefits until the technique becomes familiar – keep practising.
- As you do Breath of Fire, let the air make a loud noise as it rushes out through your nostrils.
- Try Breath of Fire for just one minute if the technique is new to you. As you get accustomed to it, build up to two or three minutes.
- If you start to feel dizzy, uncomfortable or breathless, take a break and try again on another occasion.
- Try to keep your spine straight throughout.
- Avoid doing the Breath of Fire technique when you're feeling unwell or if you have a chronic medical condition, such as high blood pressure.

tantric technique

kundalini shaking

Try opening up physically, emotionally and spiritually before you make love by practising this tried-and-tested tantric technique.

In Tantric tradition, kundalini is a storehouse of energy that lies at the base of the spine (kundalini means "coiled serpent"). The following exercise – kundalini shaking – gets the energy moving up through the core of your body. Do kundalini shaking with your lover – it will allow you to connect with each other more quickly, deeply and blissfully.

SHAKE AND RELEASE

step 1 Because kundalini shaking involves lots of fast movement it helps to play some music that gets you going. So, after you've done the breath awareness exercise (see page 20), put on some fast, dynamic music, then stand near your lover and begin shaking. Start with your knees. Don't just bend and unbend them – literally allow them to shake. Your

aim is to wake up your kundalini energy through fast vibrations. If it helps, imagine that you're trembling with cold; or pretend the floor you're standing on has started to vibrate.

step 2 Let the vibrations travel up from your knees into your hips. Let your hips shake. Don't worry about whether you look silly or unsexy, and don't try to dance or follow any formula – just let yourself be taken over by movement. Shake your knees and hips for several minutes. Even if you feel tired, keep up the intensity of the movement.

step 3 After five minutes, shake your belly and then chest. You may find that your body has started to shake involuntarily. If so, that's fine – just surrender to the kundalini energy rising through you. Keep breathing as you shake and do a mental scan of your body to check that you're not holding tension in anywhere, especially your love muscles (see pages 62–5), tummy, buttocks or jaw.

step 4 Finally, let the shakes take over the whole of your body — including your shoulders, arms and hands. Let your neck and head submit to the vibrations, too. Keep scanning your body to make sure you're not holding onto any tension. Abandon yourself to the current of energy rising up your body. Imagine a serpent uncoiling and rising up your spine.

step 5 After you have been shaking for 10–15 minutes, start to soften your movements. Visualize the serpent moving back down your body and returning to its coiled position as you make your breathing slower and more regular. Make your movements smaller and smaller until you come to a standstill. Gaze at your lover and smile.

JOYFUL BONDING

Stay joyously close to each other at the end of this exercise, whether by making love, soul gazing (see pages 118–19) or lying down and embracing.

shake out inhibitions

A big obstacle for many people is not the physical demand of shaking for 10–15 minutes, but the psychological challenge of surrendering control. Common thoughts that might prevent someone doing this exercise are "I'll look stupid"; "I wobble too much already"; "I'm scared of losing control" or "I can't do that – it sounds too weird."

Treat this exercise as a way to get rid of inhibitions. If you can do this, you'll not only feel more free and at home with yourself, you'll also feel more relaxed, trusting and able to let go with your lover, both in and out of bed.

As you surrender to the whole-body vibrations and release kundalini energy, imagine that you're shaking out all the things you don't want in your life: everything from inhibitions to problems and negative thoughts.

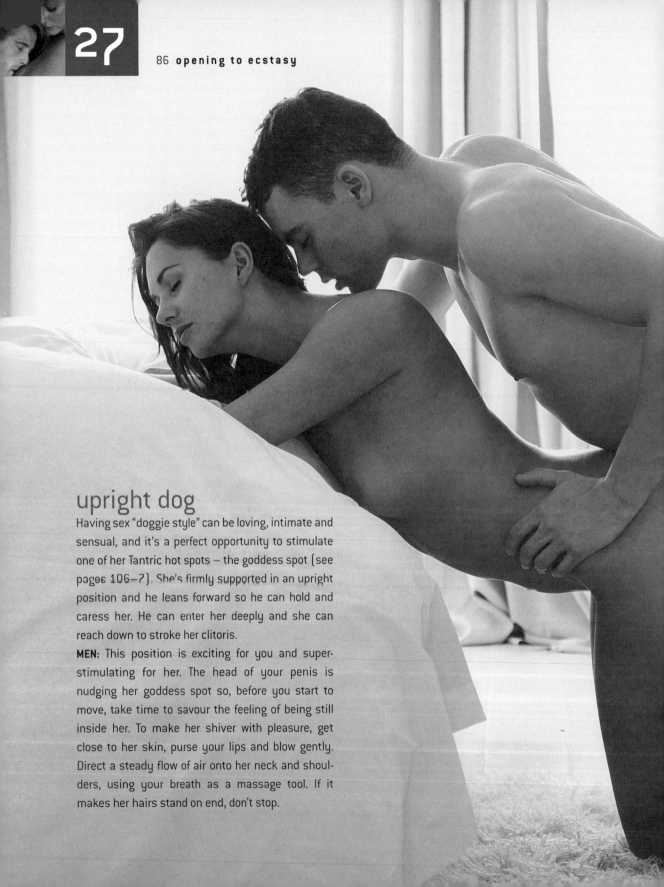

upright dog

Having sex "doggie style" can be loving, intimate and sensual, and it's a perfect opportunity to stimulate one of her Tantric hot spots – the goddess spot (see pages 106–7). She's firmly supported in an upright position and he leans forward so he can hold and caress her. He can enter her deeply and she can reach down to stroke her clitoris.

MEN: This position is exciting for you and super-stimulating for her. The head of your penis is nudging her goddess spot so, before you start to move, take time to savour the feeling of being still inside her. To make her shiver with pleasure, get close to her skin, purse your lips and blow gently. Direct a steady flow of air onto her neck and shoulders, using your breath as a massage tool. If it makes her hairs stand on end, don't stop.

cross-legged

Once she's comfortably in this cross-legged position, there's not a great deal of room to manoeuvre. In Tantric terms this is an advantage, because it gives you an opportunity to practise the secret language together (see page 64) by working your love muscles (see pages 62–5).

She can ease herself into this position from any woman-on-top position in which she's facing him. Experiment with ways to make it comfortable. For example, he can try putting his hands under her buttocks to reduce some of the weight on his pelvis. Or he can bend his legs so that she can lean back and rest on his thighs.

WOMEN: If you find that this position isn't comfortable or pleasurable, modify it by putting one foot on the floor or the bed.

ascending position

Although this is a great position for passionate lovemaking, build up the ecstasy gradually. Start off with a loving cuddle — stroke each other's face and body and gaze into each other's eyes. There's no rush to have sex and there's nothing else you're supposed to be doing. Just concentrate on savouring the intimacy you have right now.

Build it up by breathing in time together. Then, when it feels completely natural to do so, he can climb on top and enter her in the missionary position. She then pushes her pelvis as high in the air as is comfortable. He lets his body be raised by her movement.

Because her hips are off the ground, you can both make the moves. She can thrust upward, or wiggle or undulate her pelvis. He can thrust downward, bumping and thrusting into her as she moves upward.

losing control

Many Tantric practices are slow and contained, but the spiritual teacher, Osho, suggested that lovers should, sometimes, experiment with losing control and moving as if possessed during sex.

The Ascending Position is a good opportunity to try this because you're both free to move. Do it in a place where you have plenty of room and, as you tap into intense feelings, let your movements become increasingly wild and unconstrained. Writhe against each other. Let your genitals bump, crash and collide. Roll into other positions. Forget all the images you have in your head of what sex should look like.

As Osho says: "Forget everything and get involved in it, in your totality ... Become non-thinking. Only then does the awareness happen that you have become one with someone."

tantric touch
yoni caress

Let her drift off on waves of sensual ecstasy as you give your lover this Tantric yoni massage. Meanwhile you can experience the intense arousal that comes from freely giving pleasure.

Begin with a short Tantric ritual: place one hand on her yoni and one hand on her heart. Let your hands rest here for a couple of minutes. The continued gentle pressure of your palms will give her a delicious sense of awareness of these two parts of her body. Breathe into your heart chakra (see page 23) and ask your lover to do the same. Feel a sense of love expanding in your chest.

EXPLORE HER YONI

Slowly begin to explore her yoni with your fingertips. Don't rush to stimulate her clitoris or vagina – as always in Tantric sex, the aim is to explore and arouse rather than get to a quick erotic peak. Use your fingers creatively. For example, stroke, tickle, tug and pinch her labia; press her U-spot (the sensitive area around her urethral opening); make detours to stroke her inner thighs or her pubic mound; draw oval shapes with your finger around her clitoris at one end and her perineum at the other end.

Move your fingertip incredibly slowly around her entire yoni (pause at her vaginal entrance to pick up her natural moisture and spread it around). Touch her with a sense of loving reverence. Let yourself be completely and utterly absorbed in exploration.

TEASE HER CLITORIS

Wait until your lover is very aroused before you touch her clitoris, then tease it gently with the tip of your finger. Try different types of touch: slide your fingers in circles around her clitoral hood, tickle the clitoral head with your fingertip or clamp her clitoris between your forefinger and middle finger, and then wiggle your fingers against one another.

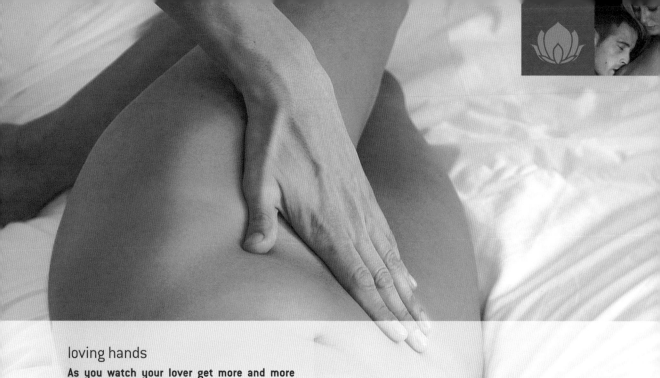

loving hands

As you watch your lover get more and more aroused, you'll probably feel incredibly turned on, too. If you find that you're distracted by the desire for intercourse and orgasm, try channelling your desire in a positive way. Concentrate on taking all the hot and tingling sexual energy from your erect penis and inhale it up into your chest (the home of your heart chakra – see page 23). Imagine it surging up through your body on each inhalation.

As you exhale, picture all the heat, passion and love flowing from your heart chakra down your arms. When you're caressing your lover's yoni, imagine that you're pouring erotic energy into her through your fingertips. Keep up this breathing technique for the length of the massage, taking her to new heights of erotic joy in the process.

"Touch her with a sense of loving reverence. Let yourself be completely and utterly absorbed in exploration."

tantric touch
lingam caress

Men love this Tantric lingam massage. Instead of the quick up and down strokes he'd normally use during masturbation, you're going to slow things down Tantric style, and tease, caress and explore the whole of his genital area.

When he's lying comfortably on his back, gently place one hand on his lingam and the other on his heart. This connects the two of you. Gaze lovingly at him, breathe into your heart chakra (see page 23) and encourage your lover to do the same. Relax and remember that orgasm is optional – it's not the goal.

WARM UP

Oil your hands, then position his lingam so it points towards his head. Use a long, firm hand-over-hand technique to stroke it and draw the tip of his lingam up towards his navel. Include his balls in your strokes. After a minute or so, change the tempo of the massage from firm and grounding to something

more erotic by slightly reducing the pressure of your hands. Keep reducing the pressure in increments so that after a few minutes your strokes are featherlight and teasingly erotic. Check you're still breathing into your heart chakra and that your lover is too. If his breaths have quickened with sexual arousal, kiss his lips, then breathe slowly and deeply near his ear – use your breath as a tool to calm his breathing.

GO DEEPER

Imagine loving energy flowing from your heart into your fingertips and manifesting itself in caresses. Intuit how your lover's body wants to be touched. Use your oiled fingers to explore every bit of his lingam – the glans, the underside of his shaft, the base where his lingam joins his body. Let yourself get carried away. Add your lips and tongue as massage tools if you feel like it. Try any or all of these strokes, or just go with the erotic flow and let your

hands move spontaneously. Be aware of and respond to your lover's feedback.

- Flutter your fingertips in soft barely-there movements over his entire genital area – lingam, balls and perineum.
- Interlink your oiled fingers around your lover's shaft so that your thumbs are aligned on the underside of his lingam. Now he's completely enclosed in your hands, move them slowly up and down. Press the pads of your thumbs against his frenulum, near the end of his lingam, as they pass this sensitive spot.
- Move your fingertips in small circular strokes on every part of his perineum – explore his external P-spot (see pages 104–5). As you press his P-spot, ask him to contract his love muscles and breathe in. As you release the pressure, ask him to relax and breathe out.
- Press the shaft of his lingam between your flat palms and then rub them slowly together.

"If his breaths have quickened with sexual arousal, lean over him, kiss his lips, then breathe slowly and deeply near his ear – use your breath as a tool to calm his breathing."

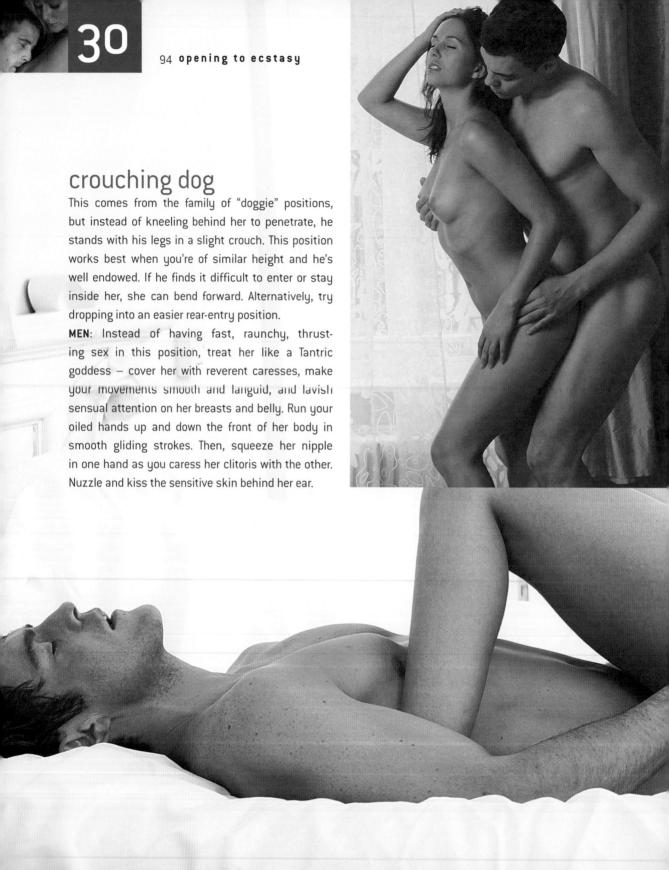

crouching dog

This comes from the family of "doggie" positions, but instead of kneeling behind her to penetrate, he stands with his legs in a slight crouch. This position works best when you're of similar height and he's well endowed. If he finds it difficult to enter or stay inside her, she can bend forward. Alternatively, try dropping into an easier rear-entry position.

MEN: Instead of having fast, raunchy, thrusting sex in this position, treat her like a Tantric goddess – cover her with reverent caresses, make your movements smooth and languid, and lavish sensual attention on her breasts and belly. Run your oiled hands up and down the front of her body in smooth gliding strokes. Then, squeeze her nipple in one hand as you caress her clitoris with the other. Nuzzle and kiss the sensitive skin behind her ear.

the pathway

This slow and sensual position can bring ecstatic results if you tap into your sexual energy. He lies down on his back and she straddles him in a facing position with her legs on either side of his waist. Then, she leans back on her hands and very slowly lowers herself into a lying position so that her head is positioned between his feet (this means that his lingam is bending in an unusual direction, so take care). She can straighten her legs or keep them bent. If she can't stretch right back, she can lean back on her elbows instead – whatever feels comfortable.

Once you're in position, do the chakra breathing exercise on pages 28–9 – this will allow you to concentrate on the gorgeous flow of sexual energy through your body. Amplify all your warm and tingling sensations with the power of your breath. Add some love muscle contractions (see pages 62–5) to heighten the experience even further.

lotus flower

She's on top in a sexy straddling position as he sits or lies beneath her. Unlike some woman-on-top positions in which she makes all the moves, the man plays an active role in Lotus Flower. His knees are bent so she can lean back on his thighs, and his upper body is raised so he can lick, nibble, kiss and nuzzle her. His hands are free to caress her breasts, belly, buttocks and thighs.

WOMEN: Tune in to the sensations in your genitals and pelvis as you experiment with different movements. Try leaning back on his thighs, relaxing your body and flicking your hips back and forth. Or try moving vertically up and down on his shaft. Alternatively, just enclose him and make all your movements internal. Your hands are free, so it's easy to add clitoral stimulation whenever you want.

MEN: Make sure you're comfortable so you can concentrate on giving and receiving pleasure. Keep your eyes open so you can watch your lover moving on top of you. Drink in the sight of her naked body and breasts. Enjoy the erotic pleasure building on her face.

breast worship

Lotus Flower is a perfect position for him to worship her breasts.

MEN: Lean into her body and take her nipples into your mouth. Swirl your tongue on them in soft circles. Moan your appreciation. Tell her how much you adore her breasts. Cup them in your hands as you plant kisses all over them. Lick them, then purse your lips and blow a soft stream of air onto her nipples.

WOMEN: Shift your consciousness from the sensations in your clitoris and vagina, and focus solely on the feelings in your breasts and nipples. The centre of love – your heart chakra (see page 23) – lies between your breasts. Feel yourself generating and radiating love from this area as your partner caresses, licks and kisses you.

tantric technique
shiva dance

One of the most exciting aspects of Tantra is that it allows men and women to get deeply in touch with their masculine and feminine selves (in Tantra masculine energy is represented by the Indian god Shiva and feminine energy by the Indian goddess Shakti). Dance is one of the main Tantric routes to doing this, and it can feel particularly liberating for men to express raw energy through movement without any pressure to perform or impress.

Try this Shiva dance by yourself first – treat it as an experiment in giving yourself up to pure self-expression – then, later, share your dancing with your lover.

WARM UP
Start with a warm-up session in which you leave your day and any stresses behind, and concentrate on the present moment. Close your eyes, bend your knees slightly, keep your spine straight and relax your belly and buttocks. Bring your attention to the connection between your feet and the ground. Get a feeling of being rooted and grounded.

Breathe in and imagine that you're drawing breath from the earth itself – let the breath come up through your feet and legs, enter your belly and travel all the way up to the crown of your head. Move your body as your breath travels upward – let your body sway, ripple, or move in any way that comes naturally to you.

LOSE YOURSELF IN DANCE
When you feel relaxed and grounded, you're ready to unleash your energy in dance.

step 1 Choose a piece of music that you like; preferably something tribal with a rhythmic drumbeat that you can lose yourself in. If your lover is watching, you can bow to her with a "Namaste gesture" (see page 15) before you start dancing.

step 2 Close your eyes and give all of your attention to the music. Don't plan your moves – just let them erupt. If you're not sure how to move, start by standing with your knees bent, and slowly circle your hips as though you're polishing the inside of a cylinder. Then, as the music infects your body, let yourself go.

step 3 Find your masculine power and express it in movement – stamp your feet, jump, punch the air, shake your arms and your body. Tap into your most animalistic qualities. Make a noise or shout if you feel like it. Try moving like a warrior or a hunter; or picture yourself as Shiva, the Lord of Creation. Above all, don't try to contain or moderate yourself – the point is to access raw masculinity and reveal your wildest self. If your lover is watching, make eye contact with her as you dance. Draw her in with your gaze, but don't change any of your movements in an attempt to please or seduce her. Keep dancing with abandon.

a lovers' dance

Invite your lover to dance with you.

- **Take turns to lead, and mirror each other's moves, holding each other's gaze as you do so. As you dance be aware of your masculine and feminine energies and how they interact.**

- **Let your movements express a sense of wildness – whether that means undulating and writhing from head to toe or jumping in the air and whooping. Let the movement and sound take you into a trance-like state in which you're completely immersed in the moment.**

- **When you feel "danced out" put your arms around each other, synchronize your breathing and slowly return to reality.**

- **Sitting in the Yab Yum position (see pages 130–31) or lying in the Star Position (see pages 144–5) is another good way to "come down" from the high of dancing.**

tantric technique
shakti dance

Find your inner goddess through dance. Dancing not only helps you tap into your sexy feminine power, it also captivates and seduces your lover.

Like many things in Tantra, technique is less important than attitude. It's the spirit in which you dance that will take you into a heightened, sensual state and mesmerize your lover.

When you try the following exercise, forget about specific steps and moves – instead, find your flow. Trust your body to take over and move in whatever way it likes. And don't worry about what your lover is thinking – once your sexy goddess emerges, he'll naturally be seduced. Alternatively, try doing the Shakti dance alone.

WARM UP
Because it's difficult to accelerate from zero to wild abandon, it's a good idea to warm up before you dance. Take refuge in your erotic sanctuary and spend time getting out of your thinking mind and into your body: try doing the Breath of Fire (see pages 82–3) or kundalini shaking (see pages 84–5) techniques as part of your warm-up routine.

LOSE YOURSELF IN DANCE
step 1 You can start your dance with a "Namaste" ritual with your lover (see page 15), or you can simply stand up, bend your knees and begin moving your hips to the music. Dance to your favourite piece of rhythmically seductive music.

step 2 Until you find your flow, keep your feet still on the floor and concentrate on your belly and your hips – breathe into these areas and let all your movements emanate from here. Move your hips in slow circles and figures of eight.

step 3 As the music gathers momentum inside your body, start making circles with other parts of your body too: your head, shoulders and arms.

Imagine you're completely immersed in soft bubbles – use your hands to make rippling shapes and patterns in them. Imagine everything, including you, is fluid. Dance with your whole body. Be aware that your lover is watching, but dance for yourself rather than for him.

step 4 When you feel as though you've relaxed into the music, move in whatever way you want to. Make your dance overtly sexy if you wish. Move around the room and take up as much space as you like. Make eye contact with your lover and hold his gaze as you dance. Give him the gift of your unselfconscious movement – but keep pleasing yourself rather than trying to please him.

If you lose the flow at any point during the dance, close your eyes, centre yourself with your hands on your belly and move in circles until you pick up the thread of the music again. Dance with your lover if you so wish (see page 99).

"Don't worry about what your lover is thinking; once your sexy goddess emerges, he'll naturally be seduced."

ankle clasp

You may be positioned apart but you can still unite in ecstasy in this highly erotic pose. To get into position he stretches his legs out in front of him, then she sits on his lap, leans back and braces herself with her hands on his ankles. She stretches her legs out behind him and he braces himself on her ankles, too.

Begin your Tantric lovemaking with some still and separate moments in which you both concentrate on your breath. Try any of the breathing exercises you're familiar with, including simple deep breathing. Go off into separate worlds but then reunite by soul gazing (see pages 118–19). If your arousal levels fall, recharge your sexual batteries by moving against each other.

Because Ankle Clasp effectively locks you and your lover in position, you'll both need to be creative in the way you move – try wriggling, rippling and shaking. You can also get stimulation from strong internal contractions of your love muscles (see pages 62–5).

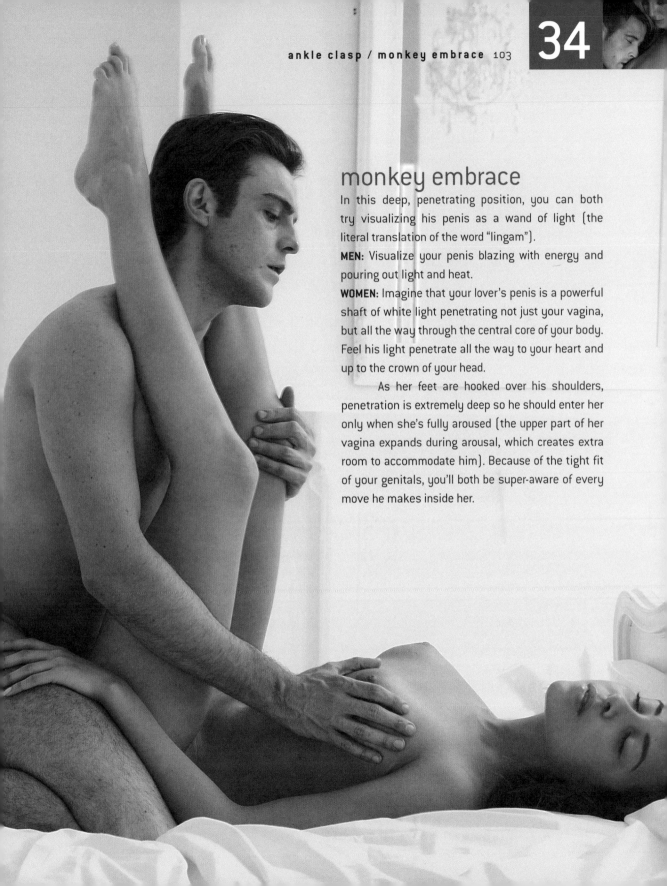

monkey embrace

In this deep, penetrating position, you can both try visualizing his penis as a wand of light (the literal translation of the word "lingam").

MEN: Visualize your penis blazing with energy and pouring out light and heat.

WOMEN: Imagine that your lover's penis is a powerful shaft of white light penetrating not just your vagina, but all the way through the central core of your body. Feel his light penetrate all the way to your heart and up to the crown of your head.

As her feet are hooked over his shoulders, penetration is extremely deep so he should enter her only when she's fully aroused (the upper part of her vagina expands during arousal, which creates extra room to accommodate him). Because of the tight fit of your genitals, you'll both be super-aware of every move he makes inside her.

tantric touch
the sacred spot

Giving him this sacred spot Tantric massage can take him to new heights of pleasure during sex and masturbation. Referred to as the sacred spot in Tantra, it's also known as the prostate gland spot (or the P-spot), or simply the male G-spot. The prostate gland sits just underneath the bladder and surrounds the urethra.

Because the sacred spot is hidden inside his body, you can't touch it directly, but you can stimulate it internally or externally. Make sure that your fingernails are short, and that your hands are clean and slippery with massage oil or lubricant before you explore your lover's sacred spot.

EXTERNAL PLEASURE

step 1 Start by stroking your lover's penis and balls, then slide your fingers back to his perineum. Explore the whole area, applying fingertip pressure as you go. Ask your lover to tell you when your fingers hit a pleasure spot – about midway between his balls and anus – then zone in on this area, pressing upward with the tips of your index and middle fingers. Press quite firmly. Remember, you're aiming to stimulate a place inside his body rather than just the surface of his perineum.

step 2 Stroke his penis (or ask him to masturbate) as you press his sacred spot. This combination should lead to an intense orgasm. Or, if he wants to, he can delay or defer orgasm and direct the sexual energy up to his heart (see page 76).

INTERNAL PLEASURE

This is the more intimate option – it involves getting closely acquainted with his anus and rectum, so you both need to be comfortable with this and he needs to feel relaxed and trusting.

Touching the sacred spot through the rectal wall is more direct and creates more intense sensations than touching it through the perineum.

As with any kind of anal penetration, you'll need lots of lube to make the experience slippery and pleasant rather than dry and full of friction. Put lube on your fingers and around his anus before you start.

step 1 Gently insert your middle finger into his anus and let it rest there as he consciously relaxes his muscles – ask him to breathe deeply into his perineum and genitals.

step 2 When he's ready, slide your finger in more deeply, then crook your finger and explore the front wall of his rectum. Feel around for an area that's raised or different in texture to the surrounding tissue.

step 3: When you've found the right spot, press on it firmly with your fingertip, or try pulsating pressure or rubbing. Ask him which kind of touch is most arousing. Combine this with penis stroking to take him to an explosive genital orgasm or an internal heart orgasm (see page 76).

why it's good for him

Apart from intensifying sexual pleasure, there are several other good reasons to massage your lover's sacred spot:

- It enables him to experience a more receptive and internal type of pleasure.
- It allows him to experience eroticism and orgasm in a part of his body other than his penis.
- Emotional tension or past traumas are stored in areas of the body, including the genitals and anus. If you massage your lover's sacred spot in a spirit of love and healing, you can help to unlock some of these tensions and traumas.
- Allowing your finger/s into him helps him relax his muscles. (Men often clench their anus and buttocks during sex, making them less able to experience subtle sensations.)

tantric touch
the goddess spot

This Tantric massage can help her unlock the pleasure-yielding qualities of her goddess spot (known outside Tantra as the G-spot). Your touch may also lead to implosive, whole-body orgasms.

HIT THE RIGHT SPOT
step 1 Ask her to lie down, then put a cushion or a pillow under her bottom to raise her pelvis so you can access her goddess spot easily and precisely. Start by giving her a yoni massage (see pages 90–91) to relax and arouse her. Once she's aroused, slip one or two fingers into her vagina so that your fingertips are touching the front wall (on the side of her belly button). You may need to bend your fingers a little (as though you are beckoning someone toward you).

step 2 Carefully explore the front wall of her vagina: feel your way to a spot that feels different from its surroundings. It may feel raised or ridged and be roughly circular or oval in shape. Although this patch

of the vagina is commonly referred to as the goddess spot, it's actually the part of the vagina that lies in front of the goddess spot. The goddess spot itself is the spongy tissue that surrounds her urethra.

step 3 Press gently on the goddess spot with your fingertips. Increase the pressure slowly using feedback from your lover as a guide to what feels good. She may feel uncomfortable or have the urge to urinate, but it should be possible to work through this and discover the deeply erotic sensations that lie beyond. Encourage her to focus on her breathing. Gaze into her eyes and breathe in sync with her.

step 4 Experiment with different types of touch, such as deep static pressure, circling or stroking. Be aware of her response to each technique to discover what she enjoys most. Then, combine your strokes with clitoral caresses. If it's difficult to get your hands at the right angle, ask her to pleasure herself while you concentrate on her goddess spot.

RECEIVE G-SPOT PLEASURE

Becoming receptive to goddess-spot stimulation is something that can take practice. If you're not familiar with it, don't expect this type of massage to yield the same immediately pleasurable sensations as clitoral touch. It can take time to integrate goddess-spot sensations into your erotic experience and to abandon yourself to deep pleasure.

If it helps, think of clitoral orgasm as a sudden, direct and explosive kind of pleasure and vaginal or goddess-spot orgasm as a slow, subtle and implosive kind. Keep the word "surrender" in mind as your lover touches your goddess spot. Say it silently to yourself. Focus on letting go of all feelings of resistance. Surrender to your lover's touch and gaze, and to the feelings in your goddess spot and throughout your body. By opening yourself up to pleasure, you can channel sexual energy from your goddess spot through the whole of you for a full-body orgasm.

lingam meets goddess

If you've discovered her goddess spot with your hands, you should also be able to locate it with the head of your penis during your lovemaking.

- The contact between lingam and goddess spot won't be as precise as when you use your fingers, but the advantage is that she's got the emotional satisfaction of being penetrated by you.

- Aim your lingam towards the front wall of her vagina and stay in the shallow end. (If you're thrusting as high as her cervix, you've gone too far to hit the spot.)

- The best lovemaking positions for goddess-spot access are those where you're penetrating her from behind. She can be bending over, lying on her tummy or curled on her side.

glorious goddess

This position is perfect for moments of high passion and abandoning yourself to feelings of dominance and vulnerability — explore the Tantric aim of discovering your masculine and feminine erotic selves. She bends over from the waist and rests her hands on the floor as he enters her from behind. If this is difficult, she can modify the position by putting her hands on the edge of a bed or other piece of nearby furniture.

Although the fact that she is bent over invites high-intensity thrusting from him, try exploring stillness in this position, too

MEN: If you stand still and flex your love muscles (see pages 62–5), your glans will press on her goddess spot (see pages 106–7).

WOMEN: As his penis stimulates this spot, relax your love muscles completely — even bear down slightly — so that it feels as though you are melting around his penis.

thigh grip

Take advantage of the fact that you're not facing each other by "speaking" the secret language (see pages 64–5) using your love muscles. This will help you to stay in touch with each other and keep you stimulated. She climbs on top with her back to him and he bends his knees to enclose her between his thighs.

WOMEN: Sit tall with your spine straight, then close your eyes and focus on the ebb and flow of your breath. Take long, deep breaths that go all the way down to your genitals. Make your breath audible by constricting your throat slightly (as you would if you were trying to steam up a window with your breath). The sound will give you something to focus your mind on so that sex becomes a loving and mindful Tantric meditation.

MEN: Breathe in time with her and sweep your hands in a caressing motion up her spine as she breathes out, and down her spine as she breathes in.

sitting embrace

He takes a seat and invites her to sit on him in this
sexy rear-entry position. He can enter her deeply and
both of you have your hands free to stroke and caress
each other. Sitting Embrace is good for combined goddess spot (see pages 106–7) and clitoral stimulation – she's free to find the best angle for his lingam
to press on her goddess spot and then she can touch
her clitoris in the way she likes best. In this position,
he can smooth his hands along the sides of her body,
fondle her breasts and hold her firmly by the waist to
pull her tightly against him.

Although you can't gaze at each other, in
Sitting Embrace, try other Tantric or yogic techniques
such as the Breath of Fire (see pages 82–3).

crouching shakti

He sits in a kneeling position and she lowers herself
onto his lingam in a deep squat with her feet on
either side of him. The fronts of your bodies (and your
chakras – see pages 22–3) are aligned.

Crouching Shakti is a vigorous and dynamic
position. Depending on the strength of her thigh
muscles, she's free to move up and down on his
lingam, rather than just rock her pelvis. Treat it as
one of a sequence of positions (for example, she can
easily lie back and he can get on top). Don't plan your
moves or stop to give instructions or make requests
– just trust your bodily impulses to guide you. Let sex
become a spontaneous, flowing dance. Once you're
in the flow, it becomes difficult to tell who's initiating
movement and who's responding.

tantric technique
female ejaculation

There should be no goals in Tantric sex, but female ejaculation can be a pleasurable side-effect of prolonged goddess-spot (see pages 106–7) stimulation. Female ejaculation isn't a modern discovery. Actually, it's widely documented in old erotic texts. For example in the 12th-century *Koka Shastra* it's referred to as *visrsti*: "At the climax they [women] experience a discharge like that of a man which renders them practically senseless with pleasure."

Some women don't ejaculate (or don't appear to); some produce fluid that appears as a wet patch after sex; and some expel fluid in a forceful gush. Modern understanding is that the ejaculated fluid comes from the urethra, but rather than being urine, it consists of prostatic-like fluids.

GIVING THE MASSAGE

The following instructions can help your lover to ejaculate, but, as always in Tantra, immerse yourself in the journey rather than striving to get to the destination. Enjoy the experience of giving her a body-melting goddess-spot massage.

step 1 Find her goddess spot on the front wall of her vagina. Make sure your lover is already at the height of arousal before you begin, as she'll be much more receptive to your touch.

step 2 Now give her goddess spot your undivided and unconditional attention (unconditional in the sense that she's under no pressure to reciprocate).

step 3 Blend your goddess-spot touch with clitoral strokes you know she loves. Alternatively, ask her to masturbate. Breathe with her and match your moans to hers. Take her arousal levels to the very peak.

There isn't a magic formula or technique to make a woman ejaculate, but having staying power helps – you'll probably need to stroke or press her G-spot (and clitoris) for a prolonged amount of time – around 30–60 minutes.

RECEIVING THE MASSAGE

If you're receiving a goddess-spot massage, the key is to surrender – if you're resisting, you won't be open to the fullness of goddess-spot sensation. Resistance can be physical (for example, you might be holding your pelvic and love muscles in a tense position), or emotional (for example, you might be thinking "I'm scared of losing control"), or both.

One way to overcome resistance is to practise goddess-spot stimulation by yourself. Get acquainted with the sensations of goddess-spot pleasure and vaginal orgasm (a vibrator or dildo with a G-spot attachment can help). Learn to differentiate between clitoral sensations and vaginal sensations.

When you feel any goddess-spot sensations reaching a crest of intensity, try bearing down. If you're going to ejaculate, relaxing your love muscles and "letting everything go" can help it to happen.

standing dog

It's erotic and immediate – he takes her from behind as she rests on all fours. He enjoys the thrill of entering her deeply and she experiences the ecstasy of his penis against her goddess spot (see pages 106–7).

Use this position to observe what happens to your body and breath when you abandon yourselves to fast thrusting. When you're familiar with your responses to intense genital friction, you'll be better able to delay orgasm when you choose to. As you approach the point of no-return, note whether you hold your breath or whether you pant. Is your breath deep, gasping, rapid or shallow? Note also whether you contract your muscles, and, if so, which ones.

Next time you have sex in this position (or any other that invites fast movement and orgasm), make a conscious effort to breathe in a different way. For example, if you normally hold your breath, try breathing slowly and deeply at orgasm.

bow & arrow

This stretched-out position feels languorous and gorgeous. She lies on her side and he gets between her legs so that he's facing her back. He holds her shoulders and enters her. Then she grasps his feet and draws them toward her, forming the bow to his arrow. As you luxuriate in the sensations of being intimately joined, immerse yourself in sensual touch.
MEN: Caress her back and neck; fondle the side of her breast; take her hair in your hand and gently tug it.
WOMEN: Slip your oiled fingers between his toes; press your fingertips into the soles of his feet; trace the muscles of his calves with your hands.

ULTIMATE UNION

chapter **4**

soul gazing

To experience the ultimate connection with your lover, try soul gazing. Using this technique, you can let down your guard, bare all to your lover and be seen as you really are.

Gazing into your lover's eyes is one of the most well-known Tantric practices. To try it, sit opposite your lover in a comfortable position with your spine straight and your chin tucked in. Decide how long you want to soul gaze for – perhaps three minutes, 10 minutes or longer. Make a note of the time, centre yourselves and make eye contact.

OVERCOME AWKWARDNESS

As you meet each other's eyes, observe your initial reactions. It's common to feel awkward or uncomfortable, and you may have the urge to look away, giggle, pull a face or just stare blankly. Or, if there is an unresolved argument, you may want to angrily stare your lover down. Let all these feelings arise and dissipate – if you wait and hold your lover's gaze, you'll find that one thought or feeling disappears to be replaced by something else.

WITNESS YOUR THOUGHTS

Try to welcome whatever thoughts arise in your mind even if it isn't the deep, soulful communion you might be hoping for.

Any or all of the following thoughts might cross your mind:
• "This is boring."
• "I can't feel anything."
• "Can my lover tell what I'm thinking?"
• "What are they thinking?"
• "They look distracted."
• "This is too intense."
• "This is making me feel sleepy."
• "How much longer?"
• "I feel too exposed."

Don't try to suppress thoughts and don't try to problem-solve or rationalize your way out of them – just accept them. Trust that they are transient in nature – like clouds drifting across the sky.

Eventually, after moving through several layers of thoughts, anxieties and discomforts, you may find you emerge into a state of mind where your thoughts seem to have less of a grip on you. This can feel like emptiness: not a negative type of emptiness, more of a relaxed, calm, spacious emptiness. Out of this emptiness can come a peaceful and loving sense of union with your lover. You can exchange a look of grounded recognition and joy.

SURRENDERED SEX

Soul gazing during sex can give you a sense of being deeply surrendered and bonded. Try it during any face-to-face lovemaking position, particularly the classic Tantric Yab Yum position (see pages 130–1).

tips for beginners

When you're soul gazing with your lover, the intention is to relax into a peaceful receptive gaze with each other – a gaze that is both open and undefended.

• The intention is not to try to "shape" your gaze into a powerful look of love. And it's not an opportunity to try to fathom how strongly your lover feels about you.

• Don't rely on soul gazing to help you recover from arguments and discord – ideally, try to start from a point of relaxation.

• If you find soul gazing frustrating because it's not matching your expectations or delivering the soul-merging intensity that you want, don't give up. Try it again on other occasions. Soul gazing is a form of meditation and, like any meditation, it doesn't necessarily yield fast results. Keep going and you'll get there.

tantric touch
blindfold massage

You can become completely at one with your lover with this sensual and erotic Tantric technique. The blindfold allows you to immerse yourself in the sense of touch as you massage your lover.

GET PREPARED

Make your erotic sanctuary (see pages 34–5) dark and seductive. Light some candles and burn a stimulating exotic fragrance. Let all thoughts of your day and the outside world drift away as you start to concentrate wholly on your lover. Get connected with each other by kissing and cuddling. When you feel ready, put a blindfold on.

READ THE BODY

Start gently Begin the massage by stroking your naked lover all over. Let your palms glide lightly and smoothly across their skin without applying any pressure. If you usually make a beeline for

a particular part of your lover's body – perhaps because it's an obvious erogenous zone or because you know you're good at massaging that spot – try not to on this occasion.

Sensual touch Read your lover's body with your hands – use your palms to sense areas of neglect, tension, pain or discomfort, or areas that just feel as if they want to be touched. Let your hand rest softly on these places and imagine that you're filling them with loving energy. Hold off on any firm or invigorating massage techniques. Just concentrate on holding your hand still and imagining the flesh beneath your hand becoming warm, flexible, pliable and tingling with life-force. Do this for as long as feels right. Then, if you feel your lover's body inviting you to touch more deeply, do so.

Feel everything As you touch your lover's body, centre your entire awareness in your hands so that you can feel even the tiniest of muscle contractions

below the surface. If you feel a contraction, make your touch lighter. Pour your loving attention into this area, until you feel it relax and soften. As spiritual teacher Osho said: "Be in your fingers and hands as if your whole being, your whole soul is there."

TEASING TOUCH

When your lover's body feels as though it's fully relaxed, open and receptive, start to make your touch more teasing. Experiment with using your hands in a variety of ways on different parts of the body. For example, use your fingertips, fingernails or the backs of your fingers to graze the skin. Again, use your sense of touch to intuit what your lover enjoys. From this point let your massage find a natural direction. If your teasing touch is arousing you both, let it head in the direction of lovemaking. If you're both feeling warm and sensual, embrace each other in a tender cuddle instead.

"Read your lover's body with your hands — use your palms to sense areas of neglect, tension, pain or discomfort, or areas that just feel as if they want to be touched."

belly dance

The sexiest way for her to get into this position is to stand with her back to him and her feet on either side of his hips. Then, to a piece of her favourite erotic music, she dances above him and slowly moves down to enclose his lingam.

WOMEN: Make your descent slow and seductive – sway your hips and circle your pelvis – and keep your spine vertical. Lift your arms in the air. Give yourself up to the music in true goddess style.

Once she's on top of him, she can stimulate his penis by moving slowly up and down on his shaft or moving her pelvis belly-dance style. She can also combine love muscle squeezes with a fingertip massage of his perineum or the front wall of his rectum – this targets the sacred spot (see pages 104–5), one of his hottest pleasure zones.

sitting squat

She takes erotic control while he sits back and enjoys the wonderful sensation of her moving in his lap.

WOMEN: Be his sexy Tantric goddess for the night. Ask him to sit down and enjoy a series of erotic treats. Start by sitting between his legs and pleasuring his lingam with your hands and mouth. Then, climb on top of him in the Sitting Squat and move in soft sensual undulations that will make him glow with pleasure. For an intimate ending, try the Sitting Squat in a facing position so you can gaze into each other's eyes. If you want more freedom of movement and leverage, just put one or both feet on the floor.

MEN: Close your eyes and focus on sensations of pleasure coursing through your body. Rest your hands on your lover's hips, but leave her to set the pace.

tantric touch
the yoni kiss

The yoni is considered the sacred source of life in Tantra. As you caress your lover's yoni with your mouth, do so with reverence. Let yourself become intoxicated with the pleasure you're giving and receiving. Visualize yourself in an act of worship – in Tantra, the female genitals are seen as something to be honoured and adored as the source of human life and of sexual pleasure.

When you give her Tantric-style cunnilingus, don't treat it as a build up to intercourse or as a fast way to get her aroused and lubricated. Instead, do it purely for the sake of it.

Ask her to get into a comfortable position. This could be lying on a bed with her knees bent and her legs apart, or it could be sitting in an armchair with her bottom pushed to the edge of the seat. From now on make everything you do relaxed and unhurried – you want your lover to lose all sense of time and be 100 per cent distraction-free.

DRINK FROM THE SOURCE

Kneel between her legs and spend some time getting acquainted with her yoni and the surrounding area – nuzzle her inner thighs, kiss her pubic area, then exhale gently and warmly on her vulva while brushing it softly with your parted lips. Then, rest your lips against her clitoral hood and begin to lick her with your tongue.

From this point on don't try to follow any technique – become completely absorbed in what you're doing and you'll find yourself responding to your lover naturally and intuitively. More important than technique is your mental attitude.

Totally relax and become absorbed in the act of giving. Open your own body up to sensation as you pleasure your partner – feel waves of tingling energy pass through your body. Immerse your face in your partner and allow yourself to get drunk on the experience of giving.

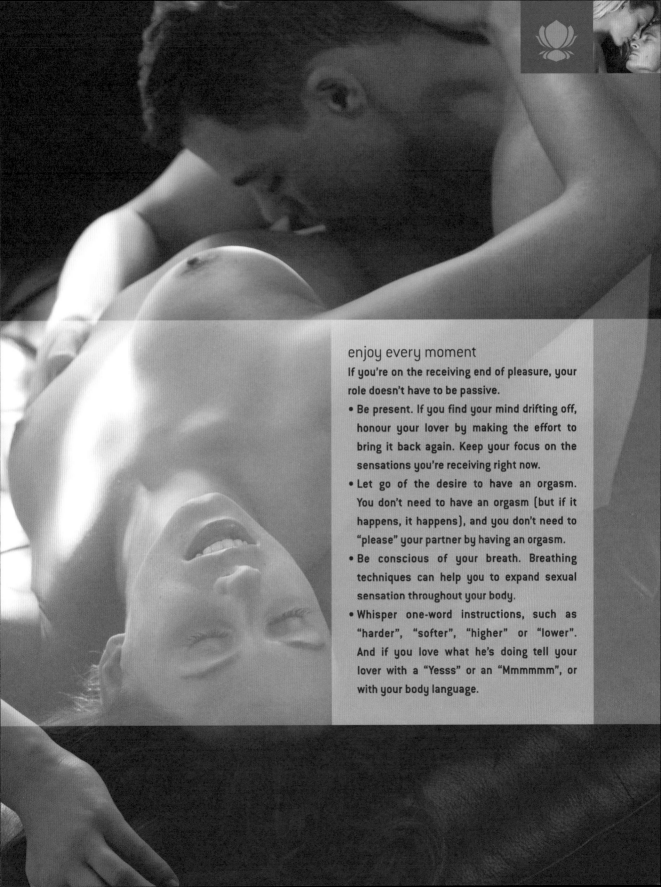

enjoy every moment

If you're on the receiving end of pleasure, your role doesn't have to be passive.

- Be present. If you find your mind drifting off, honour your lover by making the effort to bring it back again. Keep your focus on the sensations you're receiving right now.

- Let go of the desire to have an orgasm. You don't need to have an orgasm (but if it happens, it happens), and you don't need to "please" your partner by having an orgasm.

- Be conscious of your breath. Breathing techniques can help you to expand sexual sensation throughout your body.

- Whisper one-word instructions, such as "harder", "softer", "higher" or "lower". And if you love what he's doing tell your lover with a "Yesss" or an "Mmmmmm", or with your body language.

tantric touch
the lingam kiss

The approach you take to going down on your lover can make the difference between good fellatio and body-and-mind-melting fellatio. In Tantra, the lingam is treated with loving reverence, so keep this in mind as you go down on him. Experience fellatio as a unique privilege that enables you to feel truly intimate and bonded with your lover. Above all, don't go down on him because you feel he expects it, or because you want to be "repaid" in some way. Shift your focus to the sheer sensual delight that his lingam is able to bring you.

Start by getting comfortable – find a position in which you can relax for as long as you want to. Try:

- him on his back and you lying between his legs
- him on his back and you straddling his chest (your head should point to his feet)
- him sitting on a chair or the edge of a bed, and you on the floor
- him standing and you kneeling on a cushion.

FORGET ABOUT TECHNIQUE

As you take your lover in your mouth, relish the tastes, smells and sensations of him. Explore his dimensions with your tongue, keeping your tongue, mouth and throat soft and relaxed.

Become so engaged in what you're doing that any thoughts about technique (or even whether you've been down there for long enough) disappear. Follow your instincts and respond moment by moment to his movements, moans and body language. Let your mouth stray and explore other areas that are slightly away from his shaft: for example, the base of his penis, his inner thighs, his balls and his perineum.

As you forget about technique, you'll notice that ripples of sensuality start to envelop you even though you're not the one being directly stimulated. For this reason alone you'll be happy to continue your exploration and pleasuring of your lover.

"Follow your instincts and respond moment by moment to his movements, moans and body language."

submit to pleasure

It's common to be aware of a lover's sexual motivations and thoughts even if they're never spoken. A man is likely to be aware if his lover isn't really enjoying giving him oral sex, and is simply doing it to please him, without receiving any pleasure herself. This in itself will prevent him from fully enjoying the experience. If one partner surrenders themselves to pure pleasure, it often becomes easier for their lover to follow.

If you go down on your lover with a sense of joy and reverence, he'll almost certainly notice a new sense of abandon and sensuality in your actions and this will fuel his arousal more than any perfectly honed fellatio technique. He'll also love the fact that you're in no rush to stop giving him oral sex or to move on to the "next stage" of sex.

rising serpent

You can enjoy a real closeness in this seductive position even though you aren't facing each other.

She feels closely covered without being crushed; he has the freedom to move freely; and you both enjoy lots of skin-to-skin contact. Her goddess spot (see pages 106–7) is massaged, as is the length of his penis. You can make penetration easier – and deeper – by putting pillows under her abdomen.

Focus on synchronizing your breath and then breathing up through your chakras together (see pages 28–9). Give your love muscles (see pages 62–5) a good workout too – it's a great way to communicate with each other.

If the temptation to thrust to a speedy climax is too great, get into a restful side-by-side position simply by rolling over.

dog posture

This is one of the raunchiest positions in many couples' sex life. It feels primal, anonymous and naughty, all of which can send your arousal levels through the roof. Try the Tantric practice of immersing yourselves in sound — make Dog Posture a celebration of intense animalistic sex and let yourselves be wild. Visualize yourselves as a couple of animals — for example, dogs, cats or lions. Be aware of the fiery energy in your genitals and pelvis and express them through noise: growl, pant, bark and roar.

Note to the inhibited: if making animal noises feels embarrassing, bear in mind that sound offers you something to meditate upon. If you're busy growling like a dog, your mind will be immersed in sound rather than preoccupied or distracted.

yab yum

This is the classic position for Tantric sex. Yab yum means "position of the mother and father" and the posture symbolizes the divine union of the masculine and feminine. It's a warm, intimate face-to-face position, in which your bodies are closely pressed together. Yab Yum is an ideal position in which to practise Tantric breathing techniques and soul gazing (see pages 118–19).

To get into position, he sits with his legs crossed. She straddles him in a face-to-face position and rests her feet on the floor. Neither of you can move freely, but this makes it easier to concentrate on internal sensations and the flow of sexual energy inside your bodies.

You can build up sexual energy in this position by rocking your pelvises so that his penis rubs against her clitoris and moves slightly in and out of her vagina. Amplify the sensations by using your breath as a tool.

making love from the third eye

Use this Tantric technique while in the Yab Yum position and feel the boundaries between you and your lover melting away. Let yourselves merge and become one with each other.

Your third eye chakra (see page 23) lies in between your eyes at the top of your nose.

- Rock your pelvises back and forth and start to deepen your breathing. Close your eyes.
- Give yourself up to the sensation of breath entering and leaving your body. Synchronize your breath.
- Press your foreheads together to connect your third eye chakras.
- Imagine that you're drawing breath up your central channel all the way to your third eye chakra. Use your love muscles (see pages 62–5) in time with your breath.
- With your eyes closed, turn your eyes inward toward the bridge of your nose (the site of the third eye chakra). Visualize the colour violet.

tantric technique
circular breathing

Merge into blissful union with your lover during sex by practising this circular breathing exercise. Practise the basic technique by yourself first so that it comes easily when you do it with a lover.

CIRCULAR BREATHING ALONE

If you haven't practised circular breathing before, it's a good idea to build up slowly – if you try to do too much too soon, the complexity of combining all the actions can be frustrating. Instead, take a leisurely approach to get the maximum benefits from this powerful technique.

To try circular breathing by yourself, sit comfortably with your spine straight and your jaw relaxed. Take long, deep breaths and make your inhalations and exhalations flow seamlessly into each other. Now imagine you're using your breath to draw a circle. As you inhale, picture your breath entering through your base chakra, rising up your central channel (see page 23) and exiting through the crown of your head. As you exhale, picture your breath flowing down the front of your body and completing its circular journey at your base chakra.

Keep drawing circles with your breath in this way for about five minutes. Concentrate on keeping the circles smooth, continuous and flowing.

CIRCULAR BREATHING WITH YOUR LOVER

Now try circular breathing with your partner. Start by sitting or kneeling opposite each other (you can also sit in a non-penetrative version of the Yab Yum position – see page 131) and make circles with your breath just as you did before. Synchronize your breath and try the soul-gazing technique on pages 118–19.

Now change the rhythm of your breath slightly so that as one of you breathes in, the other breathes out. Instead of two separate circles, you're

mouth-to-mouth

Circular breathing can be profoundly sensual and intimate. To get an idea of the sensations you might experience, try this simpler mouth-to-mouth breathing technique.

- While you're in the Yab Yum position (see pages 130–131), put your mouths together so that your lips form a seal.

- Now breathe each other's breath by inhaling and exhaling directly into each other's mouth. Concentrate entirely on the ebb and flow of breath — try to give yourselves up to it.

- If you want to add one further dimension, she can picture the inhalation rising up from her genitals. Meanwhile, he pictures his exhalation leaving his body through his genitals and inflaming her with loving energy.

going to create a single circle of breath that flows between your base chakras and your heart chakras. **WOMEN**: As you inhale, draw the breath up from your base chakra. On exhaling, visualize the breath leaving your body through your heart chakra.

MEN: As you inhale, imagine the breath entering though your heart chakra. On exhaling, visualize the breath leaving your body through your base chakra. Breathe together like this for five minutes and then reverse the direction of the circle so that she inhales through her heart chakra.

CIRCULAR BREATHING DURING SEX

When you feel comfortable with the circular breathing technique, try it while you're having sex in the Yab Yum position (see pages 130–31). As she exhales through her heart chakra, he takes the breath into his heart and sends it down to his genitals. From here she inhales it into her genitals and up into her heart.

Let the rhythm of this breath melt the boundaries between you and take you to a place where you feel deeply connected and bonded.

ADD PELVIC ROCKING

Once you're comfortable with circular breathing during sex, you can intensify the experience by rocking your pelvis in time with your breath. Pelvic rocking builds up sexual energy, and the rhythmic movements help you get into a meditative state.

Learning to co-ordinate breath, movement and visualization can be difficult at first and you may feel there's so much to do, it's not enjoyable. If so, try the pelvic rocking exercises on page 18 in a non sexual situation. Once the breathing and the movements become reflexive, you should find it easier to put it all together during sex.

To combine circular breathing and pelvic rocking, rock your pelvis forward as you exhale and

backward as you inhale. Get into a rhythm with your lover and feel the tingling sensations of sexual energy building in your genitals and pelvis – your breath is the tool by which you move this energy around your body. Once breath and energy are circulating fluidly between the two of you, sex starts to become a whole-body experience instead of simply a genital one.

ADD LOVE MUSCLE SQUEEZES

Squeezing and relaxing your love muscles in time with your breath also helps to generate and move sexual energy around your body. Try combining all the actions you've learned to feel a joyous merging.

WOMEN: As you inhale, visualize pulling breath up from your genitals while you rock your pelvis backward and contract your love muscles. As you exhale, visualize breathing out through your heart chakra while you rock your pelvis forward and relax your love muscles.

MEN: As you inhale, visualize taking the breath in through your heart chakra and then down to your genitals, while you rock your pelvis backward and contract your love muscles. As you exhale, visualize breathing out through your genitals while you rock your pelvis forward and relax your love muscles.

"Once breath and energy are circulating fluidly between the two of you, sex starts to become a whole-body experience instead of simply a genital one."

quiet position

Enjoy complete serenity and oneness in this slow and sensual sexual position. He sits with his legs out in front of him and she climbs on top. Make yourselves comfortable so you can stay here a while (he can support his back by leaning against a bank of pillows).

Once he's inside her, you can stimulate each other with your love muscles (see pages 62–5) while giving yourself up to a passionate mouth-to-mouth kiss. Make it a deep tongue-twining kiss that goes on and on. Many couples spend hours kissing in the falling-in-love stages of a relationship, but neglect kissing once they become established. If this applies to you, imagine you've never kissed your lover before – this is an opportunity to taste them, smell them and explore their mouth with your lips and tongue. Get lost in the softness of your lips against theirs and the tender melting sensations of your twirling tongues.

lotus position

The taut compact position of her body feels incredibly sexy for both of you. To get into position she starts by sitting upright in the Lotus Position (if she can't bend her legs into Lotus, she can sit in a cross-legged position), then she rolls onto her back and draws her knees toward her belly. He kneels and deeply penetrates her.

WOMEN: The delicious stretching sensations in your thighs and groin can make this an incredibly powerful position. Even though your legs are tightly bound, try to luxuriate in a sense of softness and openness throughout your whole body.

MEN: As you move inside your lover, try the Tantric practice of focusing on the tiny details of lovemaking. For example, the way her yoni grips your lingam, the way your breath feels as it enters and leaves your body or the sensations in your buttocks or scrotum.

scissors

If you like side-by-side sex, this position might become a favourite. It has lots of face-to-face intimacy and – unlike other side-by-side positions – he enters her deeply. The fact that he's firmly nestled between her thighs means you'll fit together tightly with little chance of him slipping out.

If you haven't tried pelvic rocking (see pages 48–9) during sex before, this is the perfect position in which to try it. Pelvic rocking generates a sexual charge in your genitals that feels fantastic for both of you. Get into a rhythm of moving back and forth at the same time (just your pelvis – the rest of your body should stay still). As you both rock back, his penis withdraws a little. As you rock forward, it slides back, stimulating her clitoris and his glans on the way.

Although it can be tempting to speed up the rocking movements as you get more aroused, try to keep the pace steady and rhythmic. Stay relaxed and allow pleasure to flow through your whole body – imagine your body opening up to sexual currents from your genitals all the way to the top of your head. If you want to, try synchronizing your breath and love muscle contractions with your pelvic rocks (see page 135).

lotus pond meditation

After sex in the Scissors position, enjoy the post-coital come-down by lying in each other's arms and synchronizing your breathing.

As you bask in a state of peaceful connection, imagine that you're lying on soft cushions and blankets in the bottom of a wooden boat. It's a warm, balmy night and the boat is floating in the middle of a lotus pond being gently rocked by small ripples. Surrounding the boat are hundreds of beautiful white lotus flowers. The sky is lit by the pale yellow light of the moon and the bright white light of the stars. As you visualize this scene, make your breathing deep and relaxing. Drift off to sleep if you feel like it.

tantric technique
the erotic servant

Enjoy playing this sexual game with your lover – one of you is the servant and the other is the pleasure seeker. Then you switch over. In Tantric terms, the purpose of the game is to explore and balance your inner man (your yang aspect) and your inner woman (your yin aspect).

Although the erotic servant game has elements in common with master-and-slave-type role-play, it's not the same. For example, when you're the pleasure seeker, your aim is not to play power games by humiliating or degrading your servant; it's to open yourself up to your most deeply held wishes from one moment to the next. And when you're the servant, your aim is not to seek sexual arousal through subservience, it's to explore the joy of giving, nurturing and honouring.

Decide with your lover how much time you will spend playing the game – devote a whole evening or even a day to it. Then, decide how you'll divide up the time; for example, will you stop and switch roles in the middle of the game? Or will you keep switching roles throughout the game, say every 30 minutes?

SEEK PLEASURE

If you're in the yang role of pleasure seeker, your job is to get in touch with your sexual, sensual and romantic wishes and ask your lover to grant them. Remember, you can request anything you want, no matter how outrageous or embarrassing (your lover can always say "no" if you request something they can't give). Here are some examples – "I want you to":

- give me a whole-body massage and then seduce and make love to me
- use a sex toy on me
- tell me five things you love about me
- have a long, sexy bath with me
- cuddle me for half an hour
- talk dirty to me during sex

- gaze into my eyes without stopping
- dribble champagne into my mouth from yours
- tie my wrists together and stroke me
- worship me with your body
- kiss me without stopping
- pay me compliments while we have sex
- massage me with your breasts
- have sex with me on the table.

As your lover grants your requests, allow yourself to be swept away by pleasure. Share your appreciative moans with your erotic servant.

SERVE UP PLEASURE

If you're in the yin role of erotic servant, relish the opportunity to give selflessly. If there's an act you feel you can't do, tell your lover with compassion (see right). Then, devote yourself to doing everything else wholeheartedly. Discover that giving can be equally – or more – erotic than receiving.

the art of saying "no"

If you're in the yin role of erotic servant and you're asked to do something you're not comfortable with, it's fine to say "no" to your lover. But, before you turn them down, take a moment to ask yourself whether you're saying "no" out of habit. Ask yourself whether you could usefully push back your boundaries on this occasion. Could you take pleasure in granting your lover's wish?

If the answer is still "no", rather than rejecting your lover (or being angry or complaining about the nature of the request), try one of these responses:

- I'm not able to do "X", but I can do "Y" instead.
- Can I pleasure you in a different way?
- I wish I could do what you want, but it doesn't feel right at the moment.

"When you're the servant, your aim is not to seek sexual arousal through subservience; it's to explore the joy of giving, nurturing and honouring."

GET INTO CHARACTER

The erotic servant game works best when you both surrender to your respective roles. This makes the game more enjoyable, and has the power to enhance sex generally – if both of you are completely comfortable playing both masculine or feminine roles, lots of erotic possibilities open up.

In the erotic servant game, you're no longer restricted to gender stereotypes: he can be soft, passive and nurturing and she can be commanding, dynamic and dominant.

LEAVE YOUR COMFORT ZONE

You may find it's fairly easy to play one role, but struggle when you have to switch. Women may be more at ease with the yin role – giving, nurturing and honouring – but have difficulty with the yang role – asking, desiring and directing. And, for men, the reverse may be true.

WOMEN: When you play the yang role, it can be tempting to ask only for things you think your lover will find easy to give, or things you consider reasonable or acceptable. Instead, extend your boundaries by going inside yourself and asking for what you truly want, even if it's difficult and even if – and this is many people's fear – your lover says "no". The valuable experience is not just to get your wishes granted, but to open yourself up to your deepest desires and allow yourself to express them.

MEN: When you play the yin role, you may struggle with doing what is asked or with giving an unconditional "yes". Rather than surrendering to your lover's wishes, you may hold something back, privately resenting your lover or being critical of her requests. Instead of being half-hearted, set yourself the challenge of leaving your ego behind and accessing the part of yourself that's willing to give unconditionally. Treat it as a voyage of self-discovery.

star position

This challenging position unites you and your lover in a novel way. He lies on his back and she guides his penis into her as she straddles him in a deep squat. From here she leans back until she's lying with her head between his feet. You both open your legs and grasp each other's feet. As you sink into a deep relaxation, breathe into the sexual charge that's in your genitals. Breathe it up into your body so that you can feel ripples of energy coursing through you.

This position can also be used in a non-sexual way – it's a great posture to lie in after you've done a Tantric breathing exercise with your lover. (Her bottom rests on the floor between his legs rather than being raised on his abdomen.) Your bodies make the shape of a circle or mandala, and energy can circulate easily through your open chakras (see pages 22–3).

standing bond

This powerful and intimate position is a strong expression of traditional masculine and feminine principles: she feels completely held and supported in his arms; he feels strong, powerful and protective. Give yourself up to feelings of profound masculinity and femininity – the ultimate aim of Tantra is the joyous union of Shiva and Shakti (see page 9).

Although this position is very appealing to most men and women, remember: men don't have to embody the masculine principle, just as women don't have to embody the feminine. In other words, women can be dominant during sex and men can be receptive. This position is easiest when there's a wall available to give you support.

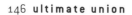

tantric ritual
oil play

Tantric sex is about playing together and taking joy in each other's body. If you want a combination of sensual play, sex and massage, nothing beats this oil slide. Make your bodies slick with oil, then slip and slide into blissful abandon.

GET PREPARED

Prepare your erotic sanctuary by covering the floor. That way you can roll around to your heart's content without worrying about the post-play clean-up, and you won't be tempted to skimp on the oil. Try thick, overlapping towels on the floor or a special PVC play sheet (most online sex stores sell them). Next, fill a large squeezable bottle with massage oil and immerse it in hot water. Now you're all set to slide.

Take turns to oil each other all over. Do this in any way you like: playfully, by standing astride your lover and squirting them; sensually, by massaging the oil into their skin with your hands; or provoca-

tively, by drizzling the oil onto their erogenous zones. Leave no body part untouched – include the hair and the scalp. Ask your partner to lie on their back and, having checked that their body is slick with oil, kneel between their legs and slide yourself on top.

Caution – because your oiled skin offers so little friction, you can slide at quite a speed on your lover's body. To avoid bumps and bruises, use your hands on the floor to support yourself.

SKIN-TO-SKIN MASSAGE

Use your whole body as a massage tool, being as creative as you can. Take it in turns to be the giver and receiver.

• Rub your oiled head against your lover's genitals.
• Slide up and down on the front of your lover.
• Sit astride them and then slide down their thighs.
• Roll your lover over and slide your chest/breasts over their buttocks.

- Slide your feet up the backs of their thighs while sitting between their feet
- Dive along their body starting at the feet and then again starting at the head.
- Balance on top of them, then let yourself slide off onto the floor.

Now slip and slide in unison. Forget that this started out as a massage and give yourself up to pure hedonistic play. No one is in charge anymore. Forget that you're responsible adults and picture yourselves as a couple of playful seals sliding, tumbling and frolicking. Squeeze more oil onto each other to keep your skin as slippery as possible.

Explore every possible way of moving. At this point it's easy to start having sex, but tease each other for as long as possible before you surrender. Or have sex that stops and starts so that there's only penetration some of the time. See where your movements take you without having a particular goal.

"It's easy to start having sex, but tease each other for as long as possible before you surrender."

mounted yantra

He's in control and can move freely in this erotically charged position; she's passive and pressed into position by the weight of his body. She can enjoy feeling vulnerable, while he can relish being dominant.

　　Mounted Yantra is powerfully erotic, but rather than racing to an explosive orgasm, try to stretch out the eroticism so that it fills your whole body and brings a sense of rippling ecstasy.

MEN: Move slowly so the length of your penis caresses every bit of her vagina from the entrance to the deepest part. Keep your body relaxed to avoid the build up of muscular tension that takes you to orgasm. A good way to still your mind is to gaze into your lover's eyes without breaking eye contact (see pages 118–19).

WOMEN: You can help your lover to relax by letting all the tension go from your own body. Imagine your body opening up to him as you return his gaze.

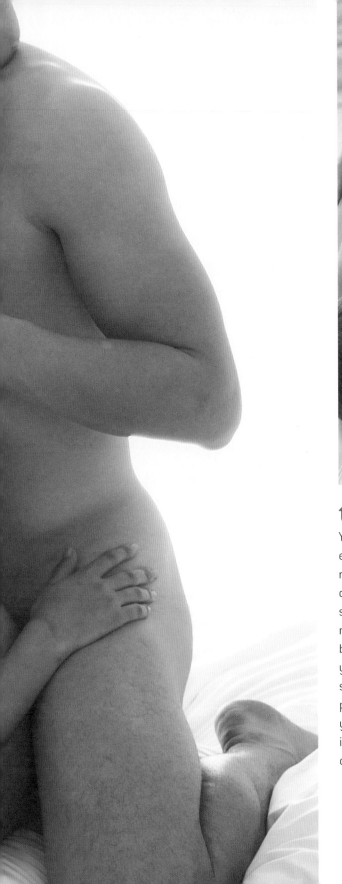

the clasp

You both lie side by side in a profoundly intimate embrace. The Clasp gives you a wonderful opportunity to silently appreciate each other. Gaze into each other's eyes and stroke each other. Let your tender side emerge. Focus on the sensation of your breath mingling, and the sensations of your naked body being held and stroked. Feel arousal ripple through you – let it spread from your genitals. If your mind starts to wander, try the chakra breathing exercise on pages 28–9 – this will still your thoughts and bring you home to your body. Imagine that you're melting together as you make love – become totally at one with each other.

further reading

index

BOOKS

Amoda, Jivan *Moving into Ecstasy* (HarperCollins, 2001)

Anand, Margot *The New Art of Sexual Ecstasy* (HarperCollins, 2003)

Bailey, Nicole *Pure Erotic Massage* (Duncan Baird Publishers, 2007)

Carrellas, Barbara *Urban Tantra: Sacred Sex for the 21st Century* (Celestial Arts, 2007)

Deida, David *Wild Nights* (Sounds True, 2005)

Lightwoman, Leora *Tantra, The Path to Blissful Sex* (Piatkus, 2004)

Lorius, Cassandra *101 Nights of Tantric Sex* (Thorsons, 2002)

Ma Ananda Sarita & Swami Anand Geho *Tantric Love* (Gaia, 2005)

Michaels, Mark A. & Johnson, Patricia *Tantra for Erotic Empowerment* (Llewellyn, 2008)

Odier, Daniel *Tantric Quest* (Inner Traditions Bear and Co., 1997)

Osho *Sex Matters* (Saint Martin's Press Inc., 2003)

Osho *The Book of Secrets* (Saint Martin's Press Inc., 1998)

Ray Stubbs, Kenneth *et al Tantric Massage: The Erotic Touch of Love* (Rider, 2004)

Sampson, Val *Tantra: The Art of Mindblowing Sex* (Vermilion, 2002)

WEBSITES

www.deida.info
www.diamondlighttantra.com
www.margotanand.com
www.schoolofawakening.com
www.tantra.com
www.tantra-kundalini.com
www.tantralaboratory.com
www.tantralink.com

A
Ankle Clasp 102
Ascending Position 88–9

B
base chakra 134
Belly Dance 122
body tour 55
Bow & Arrow 114–15
blindfolding 46, 120–21
breast worship 97
breath,
 awareness 20, 40
 of fire 82–3, 100, 110
 shadowing 17
 watching the 20–21
breathing, circular 132–5
 to awaken smell 47

C
chakra
 breathing 28–31, 76, 95, 128, 145
 map 23
  see also base chakra; heart chakra; sacral chakra; third-eye chakra
chakras 9, 22–3, 52, 144
 opening the 22
Chandamaharosana Tantra 32
The Clasp 149
Close Union 52
Compact Embrace 78
control, losing 89
Cross-legged 87
Crouching Dog 94
Crouching Shakti 110–111
cuddle, mid-sex 67

D
Dog Posture 129

E
ejaculation, female 63, 112
Elephant Position 53
Encircling Embrace 36
Eroticizer 33
eye gazing 132, 148
  see also soul gazing

F
Feminine Essence 37, 52
Fitting of the Sock 58

G
Gesture of Namaste 15, 17, 98, 100
Glorious Goddess 108
goddess spot 79, 106–7, 110, 112,
  115, 128
    see also G-spot
G-spot 63, 77, 106–7, 113
  see also goddess spot

H
heart chakra 23, 76, 97, 134
  meditation 25
honouring
  the body 54–7
  each other 14, 15
  the genitals 56
  rituals 14
Hungry Tiger 79

I
inner man (yin aspect) 140–43
inner woman (yang aspect) 140–43

J
The Junction 51

K
Kali 9
  Position of 18
kiss, Tantric 61
Koka Shastra 112
kundalini 9
  shaking 67, 84–5, 100

L
letting go 43
lingam 9, 27, 52, 53, 67, 79, 103,
  107, 110, 137
  caress 92–3
  kiss 126–7
Lotus
  Flower 96–7
  Position 137
lotus pond meditation 139
love muscles 33, 48, 62–5, 76, 79,
  87, 93, 95, 102, 108, 109, 122,
    128, 131,134–5, 137
Love's Union 24–25

M
massage
  blindfold 120–21
  breast 73
  for female ejaculation 112–13
  fingertip 10–11
  goddess-spot 112–13
  lingam 92–3,
  oil 33, 39, 75, 104, 146
  skin-to-skin 146–7
  three-handed
    for her 68–9, 75

  for him 70–71, 73
  water 54–5
  yoni 90, 106
meditation,
  heart chakra 25
  mid-sex 67
  tantric 61
  soul gazing 64, 102, 118–19, 131
Michaels and Johnson 64
Merging Position 19
Monkey Embrace 103
Mounted Yantra 148–9

O
Ocean of Pleasure 24
oil play 146–7
Open Yoni 23–4
orgasm, heart 76–7, 79, 104, 105
Osho 89, 121

P
The Pathway 95
P-spot 93, 104–105
pelvic rocking 48–9, 134–5, 139
pelvic shaking 67
Piercing Position 72
Position of Kali 18
Pressed Position 32

Q
Quiet Position 136–7

R
Raised Position 73
Reclining Bond 43
Rising Serpent 128
role-play, erotic 140–43

S
sacral chakra 23, 52
Sacred Seat 66–7
sacred spot 104–5, 122
 see also goddess spot; G-spot;
sanctuary, erotic 34–5, 120
saying no, art of 141
Scissors 138–9
senses, arousing the 34–5
 sight 34, 38, 55, 67
 smell 34, 46–7, 55
 sound 34, 46, 54, 61
 taste 46–7
 touch 34, 38–9, 40–41, 55
servant, erotic 140–43
Shakti 9, 35, 144
 dance 100–101
 on Top 61
Shiva 9, 18, 35, 144
 dance 98–9
 on Top 27
Sitting Embrace 110
Sitting Squat 123
Sitting Straddle 59
soul gazing 64, 85, 102, 118–19,
 131
Spooning Embrace 50–51
Standing Bond 61, 144
Standing Dog 115
Star Position 99, 144–5
Stubbs, Kenneth Ray 68
Supported Union 60–¬61

T
Tender Embrace 16
Thigh Grip 109
third-eye chakra 131
touch, arousing 38–9

 fingertip 40–41
The Tripod 26–7

U
Upright Dog 86
U-spot 90

W
watching the breath 20–21

Y
Yab Yum 43, 99, 119, 130–131, 132,
 133, 134
yoga 62
 and tantra 62
yoni 9, 19, 53, 67, 69, 75
 caress 90–91
 kiss 124–5
 massage 58, 69, 73, 90–91

AUTHOR'S ACKNOWLEDGMENTS
Thanks to Grace Cheetham,
Deirdre Headon, Manisha Patel
and Dawn Bates.

PUBLISHER'S ACKNOWLEDGMENTS
The Publisher would like to thank:
Photography: John Davis (represented
by Soho Management)
Photographic assistant: Dave Foctor
Make-up artists: Nadine Wilkie and
Justine Martin
Models: from International Models
Management (IMM), London